ETHICAL ASSET VALUATION AND THE GOOD SOCIETY

KENNETH J. ARROW LECTURE SERIES

KENNETH J. ARROW LECTURE SERIES

Kenneth J. Arrow's work has so deeply shaped the course of economics for the past sixty years that, in a sense, every modern economist is his student. His ideas, style of research, and breadth of vision have been a model for generations of the boldest, most creative, and most innovative economists. His work has yielded seminal theorems in areas such as general equilibrium theory, social choice theory, and endogenous growth theory, proving that simple ideas have profound effects. The Kenneth J. Arrow Lecture Series highlights economists from Nobel laureates to groundbreaking younger scholars, whose work builds on Arrow's scholarship as well as his innovative spirit. The books in the series are an expansion of the lectures that are held in Arrow's honor at Columbia University.

The lectures have been supported by Columbia University's Committee on Global Thought, Program for Economic Research, Center on Global Economic Governance, and Initiative for Policy Dialogue.

ETHICAL ASSET VALUATION AND THE GOOD SOCIETY

CHRISTIAN GOLLIER

COLUMBIA UNIVERSITY PRESS | NEW YORK

Columbia University Press
Publishers Since 1893
New York Chichester, West Sussex
cup.columbia.edu
Copyright © 2018 Columbia University Press

Library of Congress Cataloging-in-Publication Data
Names: Gollier, Christian, author.
Title: Ethical asset valuation and the good society / Christian Gollier.
Description: New York : Columbia University Press, [2018] |
Series: Kenneth J. Arrow lecture series | Includes bibliographical references.
Identifiers: LCCN 2017020978 (print) | LCCN 2017035360 (ebook) |
ISBN 9780231545921 | ISBN 9780231170420 (alk. paper)
Subjects: LCSH: Capital market—Moral and ethical aspects. |
Securities—Prices. | Value. | Valuation. | Public good.
Classification: LCC HG4523 (ebook) | LCC HG4523 .G655 2018 (print) |
DDC 174/.4—dc23
LC record available at https://lccn.loc.gov/2017020978

Columbia University Press books are printed on permanent
and durable acid-free paper.
Printed in the United States of America

Cover design: Noah Arlow

CONTENTS

ACKNOWLEDGMENTS

This book is the outcome of a fifteen-year long personal research agenda, mostly performed on my own at the Toulouse School of Economics. However, the results I discuss here are linked to various papers I wrote with co-authors: Jacques Drèze, Louis Eeckhoudt, Harris Schlesinger, Jean Tirole, Nicolas Treich, Mart in Weitzman, and Richard Zeckhauser. Their contributions are gratefully acknowledged.

My debt to Jacques Drèze goes back to the 1980s when, as a student at the Center for Operations Research and Econometrics (CORE) in Louvain, I attended his enthusiastic and profound lectures on the economics of uncertainty. But my intellectual interest in discount rates came later; I can trace it back to the Institut d'Economie Industrielle (IDEI) lecture about the economics of climate change given by Kenneth Arrow in 1995. Since then, my curiosity about discounting and sustainable development has grown, reinforced by my interaction with many public and private institutions that have struggled with these complex questions. In the public sphere, let me mention France Stratégie, the Conseil

Economique du Développement Durable, the French Ministry of Ecology, and various foreign public institutions in the United States (the Environmental Protection Agency), the Netherlands, the United Kingdom, and Norway. I have also benefited from frequent enquiries from and interactions with economists from Electricité de France, Engie, and Réseau de Transport d'Electricité, among others. This project was also supported by various partners of the Toulouse School of Economics and IDEI, in the partners of the chair "Sustainable Finance and Responsible Investment," and the French reinsurance company SCOR, which funded the chair "Risk Markets and Value Creation" at IDEI. More recently, Amundi and Meridiam, two financial institutions interested in the concepts of responsible finance, have also contributed to this research agenda.

On a more personal note, this book is in keeping with my own intellectual evolution and history. My father, who wrote a book entitled *The Future of Pensions* (J.-J. Gollier 1987), was interested in the same questions. He was a prominent actuary who advised the Belgian government in the 1980s and 1990s about the pension reforms that were necessary in the face of huge anticipated pension deficits set to hit at the turn of the century. My vocation as an economist is intrinsically linked to this intellectual heritage, my youth having been haunted by discussions about the implicit debt that my father's generation was imposing on mine, and about the necessity to save for the long term. This book is in line with my father's and my intergenerational quest for long-term economic thinking.

ACKNOWLEDGMENTS

I thank Bridget Flannery-McCoy at Columbia University Press for her very useful comments and advice on an earlier version of this manuscript. Finally, I wrote this book in 2016 and early 2017 as I was visiting the economics department of Columbia University as the Wesley Clair Mitchell visiting research professor and the economics department of University College London. Their hospitality is greatly appreciated.

INTRODUCTION

My baby boomer generation has witnessed the triumph of financial capitalism in the last two decades of the twentieth century. Our lives have been deeply influenced by financial variables that determined personal decisions with regard to savings, homeownership, retirement age, and even whether to marry, to have children, or to immigrate. For example, throughout the twentieth century, the real interest rate was negative in most European countries, and this implied the "euthanasia of the rentiers" who invested their wealth in sovereign bonds, in line with the prudent person principle. At the same time, it made the fortunes of generations of optimistic entrepreneurs whose borrowing costs were very advantageous. The waves of inflation that hit the Western world in the 1970s allowed a generation of homeowners to reimburse their fixed-rate mortgages in peanuts. Today, the very low interest rate policy of Western central banks is forcing young generations to save much more to prepare for their retirement and is pushing many defined-benefit pension funds into bankruptcy, impoverishing an entire generation of working-class retirees.

Financial variables also affect crucial decisions in a myriad of public and private institutions whose actions irreversibly impact our own well-being. Financial markets exert their diktat to determine which entrepreneurial projects are viable and which investments should perish. If investment projects in renewable energy can be financed—for example, through green bonds—at a lower interest rate than those linked to fossil fuels, the energy transition would be easier to accomplish. And by influencing where production will take place, differences in interest rates around the world determine where unemployment will hit most. Financial markets also impose their iron rules on countries and governments, forcing the most indebted ones to limit their investment in education and health infrastructure, for example. In the age of financial capitalism, our collective destiny is determined by interest rates and by the way financial markets penalize risky actions. The great challenges of our time, such as the fight against poverty, climate change, and cancer, are controlled by financial markets because these markets determine the differential costs of capital of the projects aimed at addressing them. In our free and decentralized society, investments to improve our collective future are driven by financial price signals that determine whether we will switch to electric cars and put photovoltaic panels on our roofs, for example. Because of the usurious rates of interest imposed on many poor farmers in developing countries in the absence of microcredit, the long-delayed investment in their means of production (e.g., a plow, fertilizer) is not economically viable, which keeps these farmers in a poverty trap and limits the growth of their country's economy. Financial price signals also determine the investment strategy of firms and financiers in research and development (R&D) and greener ways to produce goods and services.

The mega bailouts that saved many financial institutions around the globe in the aftermath of the 2008 financial crisis heightened the tone of discontent that surrounded financial markets during the twentieth century. The "Occupy Wall Street" movement pointed, rightly, to the absurd concentration of wealth and the Armageddon of collective resources that occurred in the crash of recent speculative bubbles, such as the dotcom bubble of the late 1990s and the subprime bubble of 2008, which precipitated the movement. Billions and trillions of dollars have been lost forever in investments that created no social value, such as homes built in the middle of nowhere and dotcom companies that produced nothing. As superbly explained by Tirole (2006), financial institutions are subject to many incentive problems that misalign them with social welfare, thereby justifying the strong regulation of financial institutions and markets. At the same time, financial institutions and markets play a crucial role in allocating scarce capital in the economy and improving risk-sharing. Although improvements are possible, there is just no viable alternative to these institutions. For example, financial markets impose a budget constraint to economic agents over their lifetime, which serves as a crucial discipline device necessary in any decentralized social system. In other words, no one can expect to get a loan in the absence of a credible plan for repayment—and no investment project can be financed without the prospect of a flow of future benefits.

Financial markets allocate scarce capital in the economy. In a frictionless economy—one in which buyers and sellers can trade with no transaction cost under symmetric information—they displace capital whenever an investment project emerges that creates more social value per dollar invested than existing projects. They do so in a completely decentralized way by providing price signals to market participants. The long-term interest rate informs every market participant about the rate of return of safe capital at the margin in the economy. This opportunity cost of capital tells investors endowed with a safe long-term project whether they should implement it by comparing the project's internal rate of return to this interest rate. For example, if the market interest rate is 1 percent, every agent with a safe project financed at that rate would break even only if its rate of return exceeds 1 percent. In financial jargon, they have a positive net present value when using a discount rate of 1 percent. This implies that all such safe projects will be implemented, and all safe projects with a rate of return of less than 1 percent will be abandoned. This is obviously an efficient way to allocate capital in the economy, assuming that 1 percent correctly represents the socially desirable degree of long-termism. In theory, private interests are aligned with the maximization of the creation of social value in our society because the long-term interest rate is also the cost of capital to finance a project on financial markets. In these circumstances, the 1 percent interest rate of the credit to safe borrowers induces them to internalize the social cost of capital inherent in the scarcity of the capital resource.

This interest rate also informs households about the social benefit that the community could create if only they would save more. Households whose welfare cost of postponing consumption is less than 1 percent will be willing to save more. This additional saving is desirable from the collective point of view, since its benefit coming from the return of safe capital (1 percent) is greater than the cost of savers postponing consumption. In theory, by remunerating them at the interest rate, markets align households' interests with the community's collective goals. But how is the equilibrium interest rate determined? In a competitive equilibrium, the equilibrium interest rate is the outcome of the interaction between the supply and demand of safe capital. Suppose that, at a zero interest rate, there are not enough aggregate savings to finance all safe investment projects with a positive rate of return. In this context, investors will compete to attract scarce savings, which will increase the interest rate up to the point where the excess demand of capital vanishes. The two crucial determinants of the equilibrium interest rate are the opportunity set of safe investment projects and the psychological cost borne by households postponing consumption. At equilibrium, the marginal investment in safe projects has a rate of return that must be equal to the cost of postponing consumption to finance a project. This means that this competitive equilibrium is efficient. If this cost is large, saving and investment are less socially desirable, and the equilibrium interest rate will be high.

The interest rate is the price of time. It drives everyone's willingness to sacrifice current consumption to improve the future. A lower interest rate incentivizes entrepreneurs to invest more, thereby boosting economic growth depending on the depth of the profitable investment opportunity set existing in the economy. Reciprocally, optimistic growth expectations induce households to save less, thereby generating an upward pressure on interest rates. The equilibrium interest rate balances these opposite forces on capital markets. This interest rate determines, in turn, the degree of long-termism for market participants and the intensity of our efforts in favor of the future. The interest rate fixes the tradeoff between the present and the future in everyone's valuation process. These driving forces for the long-term interest rates are hard to counterbalance, and most of the time, central banks and governments make no pretense of controlling it.

In theory, the same ideas prevail for the individual and collective risk-taking through the market risk premium. Economic growth is driven by investments, and most investments are risky. But if growth is desirable, risks are not. How does society determine which and how many risky investments should be implemented? Markets penalize investment projects that increase macroeconomic risk. This is illustrated by the fact that, riskier companies have to generate more cash flows (dividends, coupons, and credit rates) to be distributed among its shareholders, bondholders, and other creditors in order to attract funding. This is because individuals are risk averse. The risk-adjusted rate of return of risky capital combines the interest rate and a risk premium that decentralizes risk decisions in the economy. For example, a diversified portfolio of equity in the United States had an "equity premium" of around 6 percent per year during the twentieth century. This means that all projects whose risk profile was similar to the risk of a diversified portfolio of equity were financed at a rate equaling the interest rate plus 6 percent. If this high risk premium persists, this means that, in this class of projects, only those projects whose expected rate of return is above this threshold will be implemented. If the equity premium of 6 percent correctly represents the social cost of risk in the economy—that is, the welfare loss for risk-averse risk-bearers to accept the increase in macroeconomic risk—this mechanism efficiently allocates capital in the economy.

Thus, in a frictionless economy, competition on financial markets ensures that only those investment projects—whether safe or risky—that increase social welfare are implemented. Economists refer to the result that competition leads to efficiency in a frictionless economy as the "first theorem of welfare economics." However, the many failures of financial markets imply that the price signals they send to market participants are very likely to be inefficient. The invisible hand does not work well on these markets. But if the first theorem does not work even with the best regulation of financial markets, these market prices and allocation processes are not compatible anymore with the "good society" (Shiller 2012); that is, a society able to translate its fundamental ethical values into reality. This issue raises legitimate questions about financial markets' and stakeholders' oft-claimed short-termism and about their tendency for excessive risk-taking. But if one accepts these critiques, this means that economic agents are left without clear rules to determine which actions are compatible with the social good. If market prices are unhelpful in driving individual and collective decision-making, what price signals should we use? How should we value the nonfinancial impacts of corporate decisions and public policies? What is the socially desirable level of collective long-termism? What degree of risk should one be willing to accept, for oneself and for the community?

The inefficiency of financial markets is a standard argument for public intervention, from the nationalization of banks to public sector contributions to the funding of investments in long-term infrastructure (e.g., highways, railroads, hospitals, telecommunications, energy). But public investment decisions have their own inefficiencies, with fears of administrative costs, political preferentialism, and "white elephant" projects. After all, the public sector has also demonstrated its ability to destroy capital, as demonstrated by the Montréal–Mirabel airport, the largest North American airport built in the mid-1970s. Its inconvenient location and the lack of adequate transport links to Montréal made Mirabel very unpopular, and the decision to demolish the terminal was made in 2014. Other well-known examples of white elephants can be found in London's Millennium Dome and France's supersonic Concorde jet airliner. The gigantic destruction of capital, and of human beings, during the "Great Leap Forward" in China also illustrates these inefficiencies. Public investment decisions cannot be better than the investment decision rules that prevail in the public sector. But these rules are often fuzzy when they exist.

As I write this introduction in early 2017, European decision-makers involved with the Juncker Plan, an infrastructure investment program involving €315 billion, are still fighting to determine the investment decision rules for the plan. In the United States, Donald Trump is invoking a $1 trillion investment of public money in roads, bridges, urban transportation, and schools, with no clear decision rule in place. In the absence of clarification, this is no less frightening than a market-based decision process.

This book is about value. There is a vast literature on asset valuation theory to which thousands of researchers specializing in finance have contributed over the last six decades. At least ten Nobel laureates in economics have contributed to its development. The main question addressed in this literature is how asset prices can be explained. This is a positive question but a very difficult one, as shown by the poor predictive performance of its most celebrated model, the capital asset pricing model (CAPM), and its various improved versions. For example, the model typically predicts a very modest compensation—not more than one-third of a percent per year—at equilibrium for investors willing to bear macroeconomic risks in the economy by holding stocks rather than bonds. In reality, this compensation has been around 6 percent per year in the United States during the last century, thus establishing "the triumph of the optimists." More recently, various new ingredients have been added to the CAPM model to explain the observed financial behavior of investors and households. Regret aversion, ambiguity aversion, anticipatory feelings, anxiety, envy, conformism, hyperbolic impatience, and overconfidence are among these ingredients, which can explain why people—and thus markets—behave "irrationally" in the face of risk and time.

The question I address in this book is normative. Rather than trying to explain observed behavior and prices on financial markets, I attempt to determine the price signals that are compatible with the public good. Rather than try to explain what assets prices are, I focus on what they should be on the basis of some basic moral principles. If price signals drive society in one direction rather than another, in terms of long-termism, risk-taking, and sustainability, for example, it is crucial to have clarity about what these signals should be in relation to our individual and collective goals. This requires us to define these societal goals first and then to derive the societal values that are associated with them. If these values are incompatible with observed market prices, then corrective actions should be implemented by public authorities to correct the market inefficiencies.

Economics is a science that shares its methodology with all other scientific fields, such that new empirical findings raise doubts about existing theories and force researchers to explore new hypotheses. A specific difficulty in economics is that some of its subfields, such as public economics and social choice theory, require making assumptions about our collective preferences, which are associated with some of our collective moral principles. There is no doubt that almost all policy recommendations made by economists have a moral foundation, although these are not always made explicit to policy-makers. The utilitarian principles I use in this book have been the cornerstone of welfare economics for more than a century now. Their moral foundations, which I will describe, are easy to understand. Although consensus about these utilitarian principles is probably weaker than in the past, they remain standard and accepted by many philosophers. If alternative collective preferences have been proposed in the literature, none has yet passed the test of an in-depth scientific analysis, in particular to derive the operational pricing tools with which they are associated. The limited interest of the economics profession to these challengers does not mean that one of them could not one day become the new paradigm. I will discuss some limitations of the current consensus in this book to pave the way for these alternative approaches.

The intellectual endeavor of this book is made with a clear operational objective. The world of finance is excited by the new notions of corporate social responsibility, socially responsible investment, and ethical finance. Bringing more philosophy to finance theory, and more ethics to financial markets, is certainly a good thing. But I am particularly concerned by the risk of "window dressing" and "green washing," terms associated with the idea that financiers may use new clothes and grandiose words without many practical implications for their businesses. Without doubt, there are well-intentioned savers, investors, bankers, and business leaders who are ready to better align their actions with their values, but doing so is not an easy matter. For example, the European Union's common agricultural policy in the second half of the twentieth century has efficiently protected the income of European farmers, which is a good thing, but it has generated a huge excess supply of agricultural goods on the continent. It has forced the European Union to subsidize the export of these goods, produced at much larger cost than in other countries, and it has destroyed the livelihoods of many poor farmers in Africa, who were unable to compete. More generally, producing locally rather than abroad is good for local employment, but it can have the side effects of pushing more people in the developing world into extreme poverty and raising the price of food staples consumed locally by poor people. Or, forcing an early energy transition may cost current generations more than the anticipated benefits for future generations. Other examples abound in the socially responsible investment industry. For example, excluding "vice stocks" (e.g., tobacco, alcohol, gambling, arms) from asset funds offered to socially responsible investment customers would have a sizeable negative effect on the price of these assets if such funds were to become mainstream. But rather than increasing the cost of capital in these industries, such a move could alternatively make vice stocks *more* attractive to standard customers, with little or no real effect on society. The road to hell is paved with good intentions! These social dilemmas require a deeper analysis than the simple answers often suggested in the media and by the politicians. My intention in this book is to provide members of the good society with practical tools to evaluate these decisions, at least for those whose ethical attitudes are compatible with mine.

As discussed by Shiller (2012), the word "finance" is derived from the Latin *finis*, which means "goal" or "end." Financial techniques and tools should help us to achieve not only our aspirations as human beings but also our societal goals of collective prosperity, both for us and for future generations. Our actions in favor of the preservation of natural resources, the fight against climate change, and investments in infrastructure and R&D should be judged on the basis of their impact on intergenerational welfare. At the end of the day, collective decisions should be made by comparing costs and benefits, using a coherent system of values. This includes a value for delaying consumption (i.e., an interest rate), a value for risk acceptance (i.e., a risk premium), and values for all the nonmonetary impacts of our actions.

The principle of comparing costs and benefits is in itself morality free. Only the values that are used to measure these costs and benefits have a moral dimension. The existing financial valuation system is under attack, but giving up the basic tool of cost–benefit analysis would be a very bad idea. Doing so would mean refusing to put a value on some of the impacts of our collective actions, thereby leaving decision-makers unsure about the true value creation of their alternative choices.

For example, suppose you contemplate the possibility of prohibiting old cars in French cities. This decision would have impacts in many dimensions. Reducing the concentration of microparticles in the atmospheres of these cities would save lives. It would also force owners of old cars to replace them earlier than planned, which would have financial consequences. Because these people are often poorer than average, this policy would also have an undesirable consequence in terms of inequality. This is reinforced by the fact that increasing the cost of transportation raises real estate values in cities to the detriment of the prices of suburban real estate. If decision-makers have no way to compare these impacts by using agreed-upon values for life and for reducing inequality, they would be left with a difficult decision.

Now suppose that another person is in charge of regulating the use of fireplaces in homes in French cities. This person, also concerned with reducing the concentration of microparticles in the atmosphere, could suggest prohibiting fires when the atmospheric microparticle concentration reaches a certain level. In the absence of common values, one decision-maker could decide to impose a policy with a low health benefit per euro spent, whereas another decision-maker could decide not to implement a rule that would generate a much larger benefit per euro spent.

Ignoring social values can be bad for health. Suppose, for example, that an evaluator has estimated that to save one life, it will cost €1 million for the policy prohibiting old cars in cities and €2 million for the policy restricting the use of home fireplaces. Suppose the French government decides to restrict the use of home fireplaces but does not ban old cars from cities. With the same budget, it could have saved twice as many lives by taking the opposite view.

Using cost–benefit analysis when preparing for a collective decision remains the exception rather than the rule. There are two main reasons for this. First, such a formal valuation procedure can be implemented only after public debate about what the underlying values should be. This requires a great deal of time and energy. Fixing common values may hurt some stakeholders but benefit others. Lobbyists work hard to sway the choice of values in favor of the industries they represent. For example, capital-intensive industries would be in favor of low interest rates, and carbon-intensive ones would prefer a low carbon price. The difficulty in agreeing on common values in such a context leads to evaluation procedures with multiple criteria. This is a source of weakness and inefficiencies, as explained earlier.

Second, politicians usually hate evaluators of public policies, in particular when an evaluation is performed ex ante. Formal evaluation procedures reduce the power of politicians. A lack of public policy evaluation reinforces the general impression that policies are based on ideology rather than on the quest for the common good, which thereby reinforces populism. However, if evaluation procedures are transparently defined and controlled by representative bodies, they reinforce democracy. In this sense, I am deeply opposed to the idea that cost–benefit analysis is technocratic and antidemocratic. On the contrary, forcing political bodies to make explicit the values on which their political decisions will be made if they come to power clarifies the choices with which voters are confronted.

Following the first theorem of welfare economics, cost–benefit analyses often use observed prices to put a social value on the goods and services traded on competitive markets. This is the right thing to do only when the necessary conditions for this theorem to hold are satisfied. Because this is rarely the case, as we will see later on, it is necessary to develop a method to estimate the social value of the many contributors—goods and services consumed, among others—to individual well-being without relying on markets. This will be done in chapter 2, with special attention paid to the limitations of the theorem.

In a market economy, it is thus dangerous to use price signals that differ from market prices. In the real world, the actions that maximize firms' profits and households' well-being are not those that maximize social welfare. For example, if the private sector uses a market rate to discount the future higher than the normative one used by the public sector, this may inflate the size of the public sector because of the crowding-out effect of public investments in the long run. For investors and public servants who want to promote the good society, the dilemma is simple: Accept the market diktat and its associated wasteful consequences or resist it by investing in projects that markets consider unprofitable but that create great social value.

The challenge of fighting climate change provides an interesting illustration of the dilemma faced by people of the good society in a world of inefficient financial markets. Emitting carbon dioxide generates climate damages that will primarily be borne by future generations. The social cost of carbon, which is the present value of the damages generated by one ton more of carbon dioxide emitted today, is estimated at around \$40, but emitters can emit this greenhouse gas for free almost everywhere around the globe. This is one of the many reasons for why the profit of firms is an erroneous measure of the corporate creation of value for society. Ethicists who would like to allocate their portfolio to maximize the collective creation of value of their investments should adjust the future profits of each firm by taking account of this negative externality, using the socially desirable price of carbon. In other words, these investors should use a price signal for carbon that is not the price observed on markets. This would certainly make for a better society by reducing the supply of capital available for the larger emitters, thereby raising their cost of capital and reducing their competitiveness compared with greener companies in the same industrial sector. Eventually, this could reduce carbon dioxide emissions globally if enough investors were to use the same strategy. However, because these investors do not maximize their portfolios' returns, their portfolios' private returns will be negatively affected by the investors' concern for the environment. But suppose that one day, the Concert of Nations will implement a credible global policy to reduce carbon dioxide emissions. This would drastically penalize nonvirtuous firms, such that the assets of social value–maximizing portfolios would outperform the market portfolio (Andersson, Bolton, and Samama 2015). In this context, ethical investors would "do well by doing good."

Finance theory is most often concerned with the short term. When researchers in finance calibrate economic growth and financial risks, they use data covering just the last few decades, forgetting that the last two centuries have been unique compared with the economic history of previous millennia. When financial theorists talk about the risk premium, they usually have in mind the bonus offered by financial markets to investors for the risk they accept for the next few minutes or days. When they talk about the interest rate, they exclusively think about how to compensate people who agree to postpone consumption by just a few months or years. This is an obvious source of concern because most people also use these short-term price signals to evaluate actions with very long-term impacts. This is potentially very misleading, because there is no reason to believe, for example, that the desirable risk premium is independent of the time at which the corresponding risk will be borne. For example, it may be socially desirable to use a 3 percent discount rate to value a sure social benefit that will materialize in ten years and, at the same time, use a 1 percent discount rate to value a sure social benefit occurring in two hundred years.

In a sense, one of my aims in this work is to highlight the latent short-termism that affects modern finance theory. This effort is appropriate and timely, as we become more concerned with the long-term destiny and survival of civilization. Fighting climate change today will generate benefits for centuries, as will creating new knowledge, new technologies, new drugs, and better infrastructure. Determining how much we should sacrifice today for these very distant and uncertain benefits requires some reassessments of finance theory.

Economists are not soothsayers, and in the past have been quite bad at attempting to predict the future. Predicting the evolution of the economy for the next twelve months is challenging enough, not to mention the uncertainty surrounding longer horizons. But it is intuitive that the characterization of what is desirable for improving the future depends upon our collective beliefs about the long-term prosperity of our civilization. Fighting climate change would be less desirable if one could be sure that future generations will be so much wealthier than we are that the climate damage they will incur will not affect their welfare much.

We have an economic theory of growth, including endogenous growth engines, but we should recognize that its credibility is limited to describing the level of economic, scientific, social, and environmental achievements for the next few centuries. Thus, the valuation of long-term risk and time that I estimate in this book depends not only upon moral principles, but also upon collective beliefs about our future. This is an obvious weakness of this work. I limit my analysis to the socially desirable financial prices that are compatible with a collective vision about the distant future of our civilization.

Of course, "uncertainty" is a key word to describe this vision, and I will show how its specification—with fat tails, black swans, or deep uncertainty—critically determines the normative prices of long-term risk and time. This reassessment of asset pricing theory, with a strong focus on sustainable development, borrows ideas, concepts, and tools from many other fields of economics. Its foundation is deeply rooted in public choice theory, welfare economics, and decision theory. The tool of cost–benefit analysis provides an anchor for this work in public economics. Applications are not limited to finance, as environmental economists, social security experts, and development economists are all very much concerned with how to value the long-term impacts of the potential reforms they examine.

This book has four chapters. In chapter 1, I describe and justify the moral principles upon which the other three chapters are based. Chapter 2 offers an overview of the utilitarian theory of value. In chapter 3, I explore the foundation of a normative theory of efficient long-termism. Finally, in chapter 4, I examine the problem of valuing risky projects. Although these analyses can be quite complex, I focus my analysis on the main ideas and results rather than on the technical derivation of the results. This may leave some readers unsatisfied. My suggestion to them is to go deeper in the literature on the various topics covered here. Throughout this text, I try to offer useful bibliographical references for these readers, some requiring strong quantitative skills. I refer the quantitatively frustrated readers of chapters 3 and 4 in particular to my recent book, *Pricing the Planet's Future* (Gollier 2012), which provides ample technical details on these topics.

ETHICAL ASSET
VALUATION
AND THE
GOOD SOCIETY

1

COLLECTIVE ASPIRATIONS

I f we want to align the interests of savers, investors, bankers, and other financial market participants with those of society as a whole, we must first find a way to determine what actions—be they public or private—are socially desirable. Such an action could be a policy reform related to the fiscal system, the labor market, or the pension scheme, for example. It could be public investment in new infrastructure or private investment to build a new factory or to retrofit your house. It could be anything that changes the allocation of resources across time, across people, or across different states of nature. There is a myriad of such actions to be evaluated, each differing by its nature, its ends, or by the ambition of the individual taking the action. Comparing their merits with respect to the common good is thus a complex matter. During the twentieth century, economists built a simple and coherent toolbox to determine whether actions create social value. The economic and ethical foundations of this toolbox are the focus of this chapter.

By definition, an action is socially desirable if it increases social welfare. However, this simple idea brings us to a deep ethical question: How can we measure social welfare? Consider a community in which the distribution of bread is initially perfectly egalitarian. Consider first an action, R (for "risky"), whose impact on the community is uncertain. If R is implemented, there is a 99 percent probability that all members of the community will see their consumption doubled; otherwise, they will all see their consumption halved. How should we evaluate this action?

Alternatively, consider another action, I (for "inequality"), which would double the consumption level of 99 percent of the community's members, while the other 1 percent would see their consumption drop by 50 percent. Again, how should we evaluate this action if the winners cannot compensate the losers? Further, does it make a difference if the list of losers is predetermined at the time of the policy discussion, or if they are randomly drawn after the decision to implement the action is made?

THE VEIL OF IGNORANCE

There is an obvious link between these two evaluation problems. After all, both actions R and I imply that all members face individually a 99 percent chance of doubling their consumption and a 1 percent chance of seeing it cut by half. Thus, if no one knows in advance who will win or lose, both scenarios should be evaluated in the same way. This original position of impartiality is the so-called veil of ignorance.

Such impartiality would of course disappear once a member's identity (as a winner or a loser) is revealed. People who are part of the losing 1 percent will have a specific self-interest that will make their evaluation of the action very different from those who are part of the winning 99 percent. They will no longer consider the pure moral aspirations that the community as a whole should pursue. They are conflicted, their self-interest being misaligned with the common good.

The veil of ignorance is part of a long tradition of philosophical thinking. The writings of Immanuel Kant, Thomas Hobbes, John Locke, John Stuart Mill, Jean-Jacques Rousseau, and Thomas Jefferson offer examples of this tradition. More recently, John Harsanyi (1953, 1955) and John Rawls (1971) have formalized the concept in terms of economics. It is useful to quote Harsanyi (1953) here:

> If somebody prefers an income distribution more favorable to the poor for the sole reason that he is poor himself, this can hardly be considered as a genuine value judgement on social welfare. . . . Now, a value judgement on the distribution of income would show the required impersonality to the highest degree if the person who made the judgement had to choose a particular distribution in complete ignorance of what his own relative position (and the position of those near to his heart) would be within the system chosen. . . . This choice in this hypothetical case would be a clear instance of a choice involving risk.

The moral principle that decisions should be made under the veil of ignorance reframes an ethical question involving interpersonal comparisons as a question of rationality. According to this principle, it is ethically desirable to prefer an unfair distribution of consumption in which 99 percent of the population consumes two hundred and the remaining 1 percent consumes fifty if, and only if, it is rational for a representative citizen to prefer an uncertain consumption of either two hundred or fifty with a probability 99 percent and 1 percent, respectively, over consuming one hundred with certainty. The question, then, is to determine whether we can agree on some rationality principle concerning individual choices under conditions of uncertainty. Under the veil of ignorance, inequality is risk.

When people have to perform an ethical evaluation of a situation, there is some evidence that they apply the impartiality concept of the veil of ignorance. Jean-François Bonnefon, of the Toulouse School of Economics, and colleagues have illustrated this in the context of the emergence of driverless cars. One of the issues that has arisen with autonomous cars is that their computers have to make value judgments in place of drivers. For example, suppose that a driverless car is in a critical situation and must decide whether to kill the person in the car to avoid killing two pedestrians. Bonnefon, Shariff, and Rahwan (2016) asked two thousand people whether they would be in favor of imposing a regulation in which the computers of driverless cars would be programmed to minimize the number of casualties in situations of impending accidents. A small majority of respondents stated that the computer should be programmed to kill the person in the car rather than the two pedestrians. This view is compatible with what people should prefer under the veil of ignorance; that is, when they do not know whether they are in the car or on the street. But this ethical attitude disappears when the veil is removed. Indeed, when asked whether their own car should be programmed to minimize casualties in an accident, the vast majority of respondents reported preferring a car that would value their life over those of the pedestrians.

THE INDEPENDENCE AXIOM

Since inequality is risk under the veil of ignorance, it is useful to explore how people evaluate risky outcomes. There exists a classical economic theory of decision under uncertainty called expected utility. This theory was first proposed by Daniel Bernoulli in a paper published in 1738 by the Imperial Academy of Sciences in Saint Petersburg and became an axiom in a book published by John von Neumann and Oskar Morgenstern in 1944. Since then, a vast majority of economics papers involving risk—including those in finance, macroeconomics, and public economics— have relied on this theory. It is taught in most economics 101 courses around the world. All results contained in this book rely on it. It is therefore crucial to focus for a moment on its main underlying assumption, which is usually referred to as the "independence axiom."

Suppose you plan to visit Europe with your family next summer and that there will be a one-day trip to Paris during this tour. You contemplate two possibilities: either spending that day in the Louvre Museum or going to Disneyland Paris.

As you cannot do both, you must determine your preference between these two options. Suppose that you ultimately decide that you would prefer to go to the Louvre. Now, a few days before the trip, you learn that the airline you're flying may go on strike. This leaves you with a 10 percent probability that you will not be able to visit Paris and that you will instead be stuck in Rome, your previous destination. Now, think about this: Does this 10 percent chance of not getting to Paris at all change your preference in favor of the Louvre over Disneyland?

The independence axiom, first proposed by von Neumann and Morgenstern (1944), claims that it would always be "irrational" to switch to Disneyland in this uncertain context. In other words, your preference for the Louvre over Disneyland should be independent of what happens in other irrelevant states of nature (in this case, being stuck in Rome). Further, this independence should hold whether your family were stuck in Rome, Madrid, or Moscow. This logical property is summarized in figure 1.1.

Von Neumann and Morgenstern showed that the independence axiom has only one consequence: The well-being

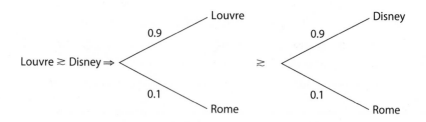

Figure 1.1 The independence axiom.

of the decision maker before the event—ex ante—must be measured as the expected value of their well-being after the fact—ex post. Economists use an ugly word for well-being: utility. The utility of an individual in a specific state of nature measures the individual's level of satisfaction, happiness, or well-being. This ex post utility, u, is a function of what is "consumed" in the corresponding state of nature: here, a sunny day in Rome, taking in the sights at the Louvre, or the thrills of Disneyland. If we indeed measure ex ante well-being by the expected value of future utility, the independence axiom can be technically rewritten as follows:

$$u(Louvre) \geq u(Disney) \implies 0.9 \times u(Louvre) + 0.1 \times u(Rome)$$
$$\geq 0.9 \times u(Disney) + 0.1 \times u(Rome).$$

This statement is mathematically correct and remains true if we replace the irrelevant alternative "Rome" with "Madrid" or "Moscow."

To sum up, the independence axiom (combined with some other technical conditions) justifies using a simple decision criterion under conditions of uncertainty, called the expected utility theory. This decision should be made in a straightforward two-stage procedure. First, for each possible decision, the individual should evaluate their utility in each possible state of nature. Second, they should weigh these different ex post utilities by the probability of the corresponding states of nature, thereby allowing them to compute their expected utility ex ante. The result is a measurement of well-being ex ante. To put this somewhat more technically, if there are S possible states of nature indexed $s = 1, \ldots, S$, and if the utility level obtained in state s is u_s, then the well-being ex ante can be measured by the sum of $p_s u_s$, where p_s is the probability of state s.

In the face of risk, an ex ante action creates value if it raises expected utility. For example, this would be the case in a prevention effort, the sole effect of which would be to reduce the probability of low-utility states and raise the probability of larger-utility states. Going back to the example presented in the introduction of this chapter, suppose the utility level in the business-as-usual scenario is 1 and that doubling consumption raises the utility level to 2. But halving consumption has a catastrophic consequence on the individual's utility, which goes down to -100, maybe because it pushes people to the verge of starvation. In this case, neither of the two actions R and I is desirable under the veil of ignorance, since the calculation generates an expected utility of $(0.99 \times 2) + 0.01 \times (-100) = 0.98$. This is less than the expected utility in the business-as-usual scenario, which is 1.

CRITIQUES OF THE INDEPENDENCE AXIOM

As soon as von Neumann and Morgenstern published their work, decision theorists began to demonstrate that most human beings violate the independence axiom (and therefore the expected utility criterion) quite frequently. Maurice Allais, who won the Nobel Prize in Economics in 1988; Daniel Kahneman, who was awarded the same prize in 2002; and Amos Tversky are among the most famous individuals who have documented these violations through compelling introspection or various laboratory experiments. A typical source of violation is when one lottery among many contains a small probability of a big gain. This situation creates a condition of regret when learning ex post that this big gain would have materialized if only one had selected that lottery. The aversion to regret is linked to hindsight bias, the tendency of many individuals to evaluate the optimality of an ex ante decision using information that was unavailable at the time. Of course, buying automobile insurance would not be optimal if one knew that no accidents would occur. But in reality, the risk exists ex ante, and insurance is often optimal. Still, people often regret having purchased insurance when no accident has occurred. This may reduce the willingness to insure. But at the same time, forgoing insurance coverage exposes the individual to the risk of a large regret if an accident occurs. These two types of regret have countervailing effects on the demand of insurance. Regret aversion and the hindsight bias may force public decision makers to implement excessive precautionary actions to limit the risk of biased voters criticizing limited prevention efforts once a catastrophe occurs. The extended duration of the state of emergency in France after the terrorist attacks of 2015 and the excessive frequency of false red meteorological alerts observed in many countries may illustrate this point. Although people may be sensitive to hindsight bias and regret, this irrationality should be taken into account when evaluating the impact of a policy on welfare.

Another source of violation of the independence axiom is the formation of expectations about the outcome of a lottery once it has been selected, so that individuals become disappointed if the realized outcome is below this "reference point." In this context, individuals may prefer to select a lottery ex ante for which they know they will form lower expectations, so that it is less likely they will be disappointed ex post. The anticipation of human emotions such as regret, disappointment, anxiety, or envy may indeed induce people to violate the independence axiom. Moreover, laboratory experiments have documented the various systematic biases of human beings in their estimations of probabilities. For example, many people tend to systematically overestimate low-probability events. Others fail to update their beliefs correctly after new information is revealed.[1] So while the expected utility theory performs well in the abstract, in terms of describing how people actually behave under conditions of risk, it is a relatively poor predictor.

And yet the independence axiom is normatively compelling and intuitively appealing. In the words of Milton Friedman and Leonard Savage (1952), its "intuitive appeal" is "unique among maxims for wise action." Savage, one of the most well-respected statisticians of the twentieth century, was one of the most forceful defenders of the theory. He published a paper in 1951 and an important book in 1954 that generalized the theory to a case in which no objective probability distribution exists. In this "subjective" generalization of expected utility theory, Savage demonstrated that under a reinterpretation of the independence axiom called the "sure thing principle," when no objective probabilities exist, people should pick a subjective probability distribution to estimate their subjective expected utility. For example, people may not know the true probability of a strike when attempting to go from Rome to Paris, but they should use a unique probability for this event when comparing the alternative strategies to manage the risk. From the prescriptive view of expected utility theory defended by most experts at the time, violations of the independence axiom were considered proof that people make mistakes and sometimes behave "irrationally." During a lunch meeting in a 1952 conference organized in Paris, Maurice Allais submitted to Leonard Savage a set of lottery choices that led to the celebrated "Allais paradox." The choices Savage made violated the independence axiom that was at the heart of his own theory! Savage was forced to publicly recognize that he had acted irrationally and that he had made a mistake. After an in-depth analysis of the problem, he claimed that he wanted to change his choice and select the option that conformed to his theory, which was the wiser choice.

This example illustrates the difference between a normative approach and a positive approach. In our context, a normative approach helps individuals shape their decision process in line with their fundamental preferences. On the contrary, the positive approach to decision making attempts to predict decisions by assessing the many biases that may affect people in the decision-making process. Savage recognized the biases that led to his mistake and corrected it after realizing that his choice was not compatible with his fundamental preferences. The problem with this outcome, however, comes from the difficulty in differentiating biases from preferences. For example, distorting the probability of low-probability events upward may be a trait of an individual's fundamental preferences under conditions of uncertainty.

In this book, I adopt Savage's prescriptive posture and accordingly consider the independence axiom as a principle of rationality. But the reader should keep in mind that the jury is still out on whether it could be rational to deviate from this axiom. If people violate the independence axiom because they may feel regret ex post the decision they made ex ante in the light of new information unavailable at the time of the decision, should we collectively behave that way? I believe not. I believe that it is irrational to judge the optimality of an action ex ante by using information that was not available at the time of the decision. For example, we should not condemn our ancestors who initiated climate change because of their emission of greenhouse gases. They had no information about the harm they were causing us. About climate change, there is much to fear, but not much to regret, at least at this stage.

Proponents of the independence axiom have developed a "Dutch book" argument in its favor. In essence, this argument says that if a person violates the axiom, they can be subsequently presented with a succession of decisions (or so-called Dutch book contracts), all of which the person is willing to take, but which, taken together, are certain to leave the person poorer at the end. The idea is as follows. Say I prefer a certain visit to the Louvre over a certain visit to Disneyland, but at the same time I prefer a lottery that gives me a ticket to Disney with probability 0.9 over a lottery that gives me a ticket to the Louvre with probability 0.9, thereby contradicting the axiom. Or suppose that I initially received the lottery to go to the Louvre with a probability of 0.9. From our assumption, I am willing to pay a certain amount to switch to the Disneyland lottery. Suppose that a trader offers to take this payment and make the necessary switch. Once this trade is made, I learn that the good state of nature is realized—that is, I learn that I now have sure access to Disneyland. But the trader comes back and offers to switch me back to a visit to the Louvre for a small fee. Given that my preference is for a sure Louvre trip over a sure Disneyland trip, I am happy to take him up on the offer. But then, complicating matters, the taxi drivers go on strike in Paris, making the Louvre trip uncertain again. We are back to the initial position where I, the agent, own the Louvre option with uncertainty, after having paid the trader twice. Violators of the independence axiom are thus money machines for traders. Repeating this operation several times will lead me to ruin. Thus, it may be a good idea to escape this risk by using a decision criterion that complies with the axiom.

It is noteworthy that utility is here a cardinal concept. Doubling utility really means doubling the level of happiness. In expected utility theory, state-specific losses and gains in utility can be compared and added up. Consider the risk of gaining or losing $100 with equal probabilities. Without further information about how to translate these payoffs into changes in utility, it is impossible to determine whether accepting the risk is desirable; that is, whether the risk increases expected utility. Economists refer to "utils" as the abstract units of measurement for utility. If increasing consumption by $100 raises utility by k, and reducing consumption by $100 reduces utility by anything h larger than k, then accepting the risk is undesirable, because the change in expected utility when taking the risk, $0.5k - 0.5h$, would be negative.

UTILITARIANISM

If we combine the moral principle of the veil of ignorance with the rational axiom of independence, we obtain utilitarianism, and more specifically, the utilitarian welfare function. Consider an impartial agent who is confronted with making a value judgment about a policy that would change the distribution of consumption in the economy, as was the case for action I presented earlier in this chapter. Under the veil of ignorance, inequality is risk. If action I is implemented, each individual in the community placed under the veil of ignorance will face the risk of ending up in the unlucky group of people for whom consumption is halved. Under this veil of ignorance, the decision to implement action I is socially desirable if the lottery of doubling or halving consumption, with probabilities of 99 percent and 1 percent, respectively, dominates the status quo solution. In other words, the welfare analysis of consumption inequality is equivalent to the welfare analysis of risk, in which the distribution of incomes plays the role of the probability distribution of risk in the expected utility model. The well-being of this representative agent ex ante measures the social welfare of society as a whole. By the independence axiom, social welfare is the expected utility. For example, if there are S social classes, $s = 1, \ldots, S$, with class s enjoying utility u_s, then the social welfare in that society should be equal to the sum of $p_s u_s$, where p_s is the subjective probability of belonging to class s. Thus, social welfare is just a weighted sum of individual utilities. A policy would be desirable if the weighted loss in utility of the losers generated by the policy were more than compensated by the weighted gain in utility of the winners.

The crucial property derived from the independence axiom is additivity, which implies that the well-being of agent X does not influence one's evaluation of the contribution of agent Y to social welfare. Increasing the utility of all individuals in class s by 1 will increase social welfare by the weight p_s, independent of the level of utility attained by other people in the community. This additivity property does not say much about how to weigh the utility of each member s. If one has rational expectations under the veil of ignorance, subjective probabilities should be equal to the true proportion of the corresponding class in the population. This would mean that each individual would receive the same weight in the social welfare function, yielding a sense of fairness. In our example, if action I is implemented, two social classes would be created, with a rich one representing 99 percent of the population. In that case, social welfare should be measured by $0.99u_1 + 0.01u_2$, where u_1 and u_2 measure the utility of rich and poor people, respectively. But without rational expectations, the subjective probabilities used to compute expected utility may differ from the objective ones, implying that some social classes may receive more weight per capita than others when measuring the social desirability of a policy.

Utilitarianism is the cornerstone of cost–benefit analysis. It demonstrates that the evaluation of a collective action, the costs and benefits of which are disseminated in a community of stakeholders, can be performed by adding up the net individual benefits measured in terms of utility. It also allows one to see whether this net social benefit is positive.

PRIORITARIANISM

Suppose that a policy creates ten transferable utils (the units used to measure utility). The equal-weight utilitarian decision rule described here means that one should be indifferent about how to allocate this utility to individuals. For example, one could give the entire utility to a single person selected randomly. Or, one could allocate it equally among the entire population. Because these allocations lead to the same average utility in the population, under the veil of ignorance, one should be indifferent about which option to select. A given total utility has the same value however unequally distributed. Utilitarianism gives no value to the reduction of inequalities of individual well-beings. Only the total utility matters.

Since a theory that can't take inequality in well-beings into account seems intuitively incomplete for measuring social welfare, Sen (1973) proposed an alternative approach called "prioritarianism," where priority is given to the worse off. Under prioritarianism, a person's well-being contributes more to social welfare if the person is badly off than if they are well off. Prioritarianism implies that when a reform creates some transferable utils, it is best to allocate them to those who don't have much of them. Prioritarianism is obtained by putting, in one way or another, more weight on the utility of the poorest in the social welfare function. Technically, it consists of replacing individual well-beings u_s with $v_s = v(u_s)$ in the social welfare function, where v is an increasing and concave function representing our collective preference in favor of reducing inequalities in well-being.[2] This means that a small increase in u_s by k increases social welfare not by $p_s k$ as in utilitarianism, but by $p_s k v'(u_s)$. Because of the concavity of v, the additional weight $v'(u_s)$ is decreasing in the utility u_s already achieved by the people to which this benefit is accrued. The concavity of this function shows our relative concern to the poorest when allocating utils in the population. Compared to utilitarianism, prioritarianism puts more weight on the gain of utility obtained by those worse off in the cost–benefit analysis.

John Rawls (1971) proposed an extreme version of the prioritarian criterion. The Rawlsian criterion consists of maximizing the utility of those citizens who are worst off. This so-called maxmin criterion tends to egalitarianism in an extreme way, since under this principle, one should be willing to improve the fate of the worst off at any cost to the better off. This is particularly problematic when we add the time dimension to the problem, as we will see in the next section.

Prioritarianism is obtained from equal-weight utilitarianism at the cost of replacing individual well-beings u_s by their social valuation v_s. It necessitates some crucial rewording and reinterpretation of concepts and analyses made under the classical approach. In particular, the social valuation v_s contains a normative component that is traditionally absent when measuring individual well-beings. I will come back to this point later in this book.

DISCOUNTED UTILITY

Let's now introduce time into the picture. Policy reforms in general entail benefits and costs that are not only scattered across people but also across time. How should we treat this new dimension when measuring the creation of a collective action? In fact, it's quite straightforward. For the sake of simplicity, let's assume for now that the community in question is egalitarian and will remain so in the future. Suppose also that everyone's utility will evolve in a deterministic way in the future and that the size of the population is constant. Consider a number of possible actions whose societal and individual impacts will prevail for the next S periods, potentially impacting many generations of citizens. Some actions will require much sacrifice in the short run in exchange for larger economic growth in the future, for example. Consider in particular a specific action that yields a flow of utility equaling $u_1, u_2, \ldots, u_S$, respectively, in periods $1, 2, \ldots, S$. How should an impartial evaluator judge this specific action? Impartiality here requires that the evaluator be ignorant about the period in which they will live their life. Under the veil of ignorance, this person will value the action ex ante by their expected utility. This is a weighted sum of the flow of temporal utility. In other words, in this framework, the rationality axiom of independence yields the so-called discounted utility model first proposed by Samuelson (1937), the axiomatic foundation of which was provided by Koopmans (1960). It implies that one should accept any policy that costs one unit of utility today if it raises future weighted utility by at least one unit.

To illustrate this concept and see the link between discounted utility theory and expected utility theory under the veil of ignorance, suppose that in the absence of an action, there will be no growth in the future, so that $u_1 = u_2 = \dots = u_{100}$. Consider an alternative action that would, for example, consist of a massive investment in new infrastructure. Undertaking this investment would reduce the utility of the first generation by 50 percent, because this generation would bear all the investment cost and not benefit from the new infrastructure since they will not live long enough. But the next ninety-nine generations will see their own utility doubled thanks to the new infrastructure. Under the veil of ignorance with regard to which generation one belongs to, the problem of valuing this project is exactly the same as the one examined earlier, and it is equivalent to determining whether the risk of doubling or halving consumption with respective probabilities of 99 percent and 1 percent increases expected utility.

Notice that the original discounted utility theory is silent about which generational weights should be used in the intergenerational welfare function. Impartiality and rational expectations suggest using the same weight for different generations, so that the expected utility is equal to the sum of the generational utility flow. Because the size of the different generations is assumed to be constant in this example, every person has an equal chance of belonging to any specific generation in the future. Thus, expected utility should be measured by using equal probabilities; that is equal weights. However, since Samuelson (1937), researchers in macroeconomics and finance have evaluated intergenerational welfare by using generational weights that decrease exponentially with time, which penalizes future generations. Doing so means that people born later in the future would count less for the evaluator than those born sooner, or than the current generation. This adjustment was made in recognition of the fact that most people are impatient. For most people, happiness tomorrow is less valuable than happiness today.

I radically oppose this generalization. It's true that most people are impatient, as they discount the flow of their own future utility at a positive rate. But penalizing one's own future is not the same thing as penalizing someone else's future. Putting a smaller weight on future generations in the welfare function is a kind of "ageism" that penalizes people just for being born late. This is amoral in the same way that sexism is amoral in penalizing women because of their gender and the way racism is amoral in penalizing black people because of their race. Kenneth Arrow (1999) is also strongly opposed to this approach and cites various classical authors on this matter. The most well-known citation is from Frank P. Ramsey (1928): "It is assumed that we do not discount later enjoyments in comparison with earlier ones, a practice which is ethically indefensible and arises merely from the weakness of the imagination." Many other distinguished economists can also be cited; for example, Henry Sidgwick (1890): "It seems . . . clear that the time at which a man exists cannot affect the value of his happiness from a universal point of view; and that the interests of posterity must concern a Utilitarian as much as those of his contemporaries"; Roy Harrod (1948): "Pure time preference [is] a polite expression for rapacity and the conquest of reason by passion"; Tjalling Koopmans (1960): "[I have] an ethical preference for neutrality as between the welfare of different generations"; and Robert Solow (1974): "In solemn conclave assembled, so to speak, we ought to act as if the social rate of pure time preference were zero."

Notice that eliminating collective impatience and its associated pure time preference does not mean that one should not discount future monetary benefits at a positive rate, as I will show later in this book.

Applying the Rawlsian maxmin principle would change the decision criterion radically in this intertemporal framework. Suppose that the economy under scrutiny is expecting to continue to grow in the future, so that utility will increase with time. This means that the worst-off generation is the current one. Applying the maxmin criterion would imply that any action that raises the welfare of the current generation would be desirable, at any cost to future generations. For example, fighting climate change would probably not be socially desirable under the Rawlsian criterion. This illustrates how an extreme—but a priori noble—moral principle such as the Rawlsian one can lead to clearly undesirable policy recommendations. The problem is not with the recommendation, but with the principle. Although I am sympathetic to prioritarianism, its extreme maxmin version should be rejected. Ignoring any impact of a policy except the impact on the well-being of the poorest in our community is ethically problematic.

Thus, discounted utility can be justified by the combination of the independence axiom and the veil of ignorance with respect to birth date. This aligns with the justification of utilitarianism and the veil of ignorance with respect to social class. These ideas can be combined into one general model. In a dynamic framework involving uncertainty and inequality, social welfare should be measured by the unweighted sum of the expected utility of the different individuals who will be impacted by the policy under scrutiny. This objective function has the property of being addictive with respect to the three traditional sources of heterogeneity: risk, time, and inequality.

SUMMARY

In this first chapter, I have described the ethical foundations of the evaluation analysis that will be developed later on in this book. An act is socially desirable if it raises intergenerational welfare, which is measured by an unweighted sum of the expected utility of the people that will live on this planet. I have shown that this moral principle is supported by two ideas. First, when faced with decisions that will have heterogeneous impacts on the distribution of wealth or consumption, we should evaluate them under the veil of ignorance. This forces impartiality and transforms the distributional problem into a problem of decision under conditions of risk. It identifies inequality aversion as a specific application of risk aversion, two concepts that will be discussed in the next chapter.

Second, I have shown that it is normatively appealing to have a decision criterion under conditions of risk that satisfies the independence axiom. This axiom states that our preference for lottery X over lottery Y should be independent of compounding them with a new common outcome. This axiom supports the cost–benefit analysis used in this book.

2

CHOICE AND MEASURE OF VALUES

The fiduciary duty of the managers of a firm is to maximize profit. The credo of capital liberalism is that this objective is perfectly capable of being compatible with our collective pursuit of the common good. In this chapter, I explore the arguments supporting this view in a static and risk-free framework, leaving the treatment of risk and time for the remainder of the book.

THE RANA PLAZA CATASTROPHE

On April 24, 2013, an eight-story garment factory in the Rana Plaza building in Dhaka, Bangladesh, collapsed. The death toll was 1,129, and approximately 2,515 more people were rescued from the building, injured but alive. The day before the collapse, a TV station had recorded footage showing cracks in the Rana Plaza building. In spite of this and other signs of an imminent catastrophe, the owner of the building claimed it was safe, and some managers even threatened to withhold a month's pay from workers who refused to come to work. The tragedy led to fraught international debate about safety standards in the country. Three years before the catastrophe, Walmart—one of the factory's clients—rejected reforms that would have forced retailers to pay more for apparel to help Bangladesh factories improve safety standards.

Hindsight bias makes it difficult to impartially evaluate what the socially desirable action would have been. After all, the low cost of unskilled labor is one of Bangladesh's few comparative advantages, and raising safety standards would probably reduce jobs the country needs so eagerly to improve welfare. Retailers typically pay around $5 for a piece of denim clothing that would sell in the West for $50. International competition limits the salary of the low-skilled workers used in the Bangladeshi garment industry, and the minimum monthly wage has remained at about $60 for years. This low cost of labor is key for Bangladesh to retain its competitive advantage in the garment sector, which represents more than 80 percent of its exports. The crude reality is that most workers in the Rana Plaza factory earned no more than the minimum wage, and that most had no alternative but to work in the garment industry just to survive; in these circumstances, how to balance the cost of improving safety with the benefit of reducing the probability of lethal accidents is a vital question. For Bangladeshi society, it is crucial to determine what will do the most good for each taka spent. Improving safety in the Bangladeshi garment industry may reduce its international competitiveness. What would happen to these workers if their jobs were moved to other countries? And rather than improving safety, wouldn't it be more useful to put a priority on wages? These questions of value should be a primary concern not only for the Bangladesh authorities, but also for all the stakeholders of the garment industry, including consumers, shareholders, and responsible investors. As of early 2017, more than two hundred foreign brands have agreed to two safety schemes and have promised to spend tens of millions of dollars to improve the safety of factories.

In this chapter, I explore the classical theory of value. I characterize the determinants of the individual valuation of leisure, health, and safety, and of apples and bananas. I show how markets can be useful in measuring these values if the markets are frictionless and competitive. I also show how observing actual behaviors helps to estimate how individuals value goods and services for which no markets exist.

CONSUMER SOVEREIGNTY

Individuals and communities have values that are derived in part from their own preferences. Individual utilities are themselves affected by a myriad of determinants, such as the consumption of various goods and services or the quality of the environment and social interactions. People value a good glass of wine or a nice walk in the park because these things increase their utility. Of course, for these good things, more is always better than less. But we know there's no such thing as a free lunch: goods and services are costly to produce, with those costs sometimes paid with the blood of workers, as illustrated in the Rana Plaza case.

Moreover, producing goods and services depletes the stock of nonrenewable resources, which implies, in turn, an opportunity cost, since using these resources to produce the goods we want eliminates the opportunity to use the resources to fulfill other desires, either now or in the future. From this point of view, less may be better than more if the social cost of delivering a good to a person is greater than the value the person gains when they consume it. Proponents of secular stagnation suggest that future generations may value nonrenewable resources more than we do, because they will live in a world of stronger relative scarcity. In this context, reducing the speed with which we extract nonrenewable resources may well be socially desirable. However, this argument would be correct only if the resource valuation of future generations is indeed greater than our current valuation. Here also, we need to develop a theory of value to be able to perform a policy evaluation.

The classical theory of value in economics originates from Adam Smith's work in *The Wealth of Nations*, published in 1776. Smith's theory of value is based on the relative costs of production, but Smith did not completely ignore the role of consumer preferences. The theory has been improved in many dimensions since it was first brought forth, particularly in terms of taking into account the existence of externalities, public goods, and market inefficiencies. The evolution of the theory culminated in the 1970s at the apogee of general equilibrium theory.

The value of most commodities is determined in part by consumers' preferences. This consumer sovereignty is legitimate. After all, if social welfare is the aggregation of individual well-beings, there is no other way to raise social welfare than by satisfying individual aspirations. If people prefer apples to bananas, or butter to canons, one can easily recognize that prioritizing the production of bananas, or canons, would not be wise. This idea rejects paternalism, the notion that some people know better than others what should be valued. Totalitarian regimes take paternalism to the extreme, with authorities dictating what citizens should like and dislike. But in a free world, it is believed that as long as individual values impose no harm on others, individual preferences and values should be taken as given.

So how should we measure consumers' values? The first part of this chapter is devoted to this question. But there exist some social values that intrinsically originate from collective preferences, rather than from the preferences of citizens themselves. For example, justice and equality are societal values that cannot typically be derived from individual preferences. Distributive justice has a societal value, the assessment of which requires some democratic debate. The second part of this chapter is devoted to the measure of inequality aversion.

INDIVIDUAL SUBSTITUTABILITY AND VALUE

Most individual economic decisions involve replacing one thing with something else. Working more means substituting consumption for leisure. Saving more means substituting future consumption for current consumption. Reallocating one household's budget means substituting some goods for other goods. At the collective level, if more is spent on education, less will be available for other needs, such as defense or environmental protection. We can use the idea of substitution to think about value. Consider, for example, the case of nitrogen oxides, pollutants with adverse effects on health, in particular respiratory problems such as asthma. Suppose that someone is willing to work at most one hour more per month in exchange for reducing the concentration of nitrogen oxides in her environment by one part per hundred million during the month. This means that the value of reducing the nitrogen oxide concentration by one part per hundred million equals the value of one hour of work. If this person is paid at a rate of $20 per hour, this means that the value of one more hour of work and of reducing the nitrogen oxide concentration by one part per hundred million for one month is also $20. Using money, rather than hours of work or another measure, is a convenient way to compare the relative value of various determinants of an individual's utility.

In economics jargon, we would say that the marginal rate of substitution between leisure and income is $20 per hour for this person. This amount also measures the marginal willingness to pay for leisure, since more work signifies less leisure. It is equal to the ratio of the marginal utilities of leisure and income. The marginal utility of a good measures how much utility increases when the consumption of the good increases by one. By extension, the marginal utility of leisure and income measures how much utility increases when one hour more of leisure or one dollar more of income is obtained. If the marginal utility of leisure is 40, and the marginal utility of income is 2, it must be true that, at the margin, one is willing to substitute one hour of leisure for at least $20 of compensation; thus, the utility loss from reducing leisure is compensated by the utility gain from the increased income. Similarly, with regard to the nitrogen oxide example, the marginal rate of substitution between air quality and income would be $20 per hundred million of nitrogen oxide in the person's environment. More generally, the value of a good for an individual is defined as the maximum price the person is willing to pay for it. It equals the ratio of the marginal utility of the good to the marginal utility of income. Because different people can extract very different marginal utilities from the same good, these values can vary wildly across individuals and across time. Some people prefer their leisure over their environment, and some prefer apples to bananas. In accordance with the consumer sovereignty principle, economists traditionally make no value judgment about individual preferences. This heterogeneity in values is an important source of complexity when evaluating individual and collective actions from the social point of view.

To sum up, the individual value of a good can be measured by an individual's marginal willingness to pay for it. It is a measure of marginal utility expressed in terms of an individual income equivalent.

DECREASING MARGINAL UTILITY

Intuitively, the value of an apple for a person at a given period of time depends upon how many apples that person has already consumed during the period. The law of decreasing marginal utility states that the more units of a good a person consumes, the smaller the increase in utility one more unit will generate. In other words, the marginal utility of apples decreases as the number of apples consumed increases. Because marginal utility and value are proportional to each other, we can conclude that economic value is positively related to scarcity: Everything else unchanged, reducing the availability of apples increases the value of apples.

Income does not produce utility by itself. Rather, more income allows one to consume more goods and services, which increases utility. Thus, income generates utility indirectly. Because the law of decreasing marginal utility holds for all commodities, increasing income reduces the marginal indirect utility of that income. Any additional income is spent on consuming more commodities. Because wealthy people already consume so much, this additional income does not bring much additional utility. Remember, now, that the marginal willingness to pay for a commodity is given by the ratio of the marginal utilities of a commodity and of income. As income and the consumption of commodities increase, both the numerator and the denominator decrease, so that the impact of an individual's income on the way this individual values a specific commodity is unclear. But typically, wealthy people value things like leisure, environmental quality, and safety more than the so-called inferior goods, such as bread and potatoes. To illustrate, the hourly wage, which measures the opportunity cost of leisure, has been multiplied by a factor of 50 during the last two centuries in Western societies. However, people now consume much more leisure than in the past. For example, the number of hours worked every year by an American worker was reduced from more than 3,000 to less than 2,000 between 1900 and 2000. In France, the number of hours worked came from the same high ground at the beginning of the century down to less than 1,500 hours in 2000. The difference is that there is a lot of involuntary unemployment in France: Many unemployed people value their leisure less than the income generated by labor at the current minimum wage, but they are unable to find a job.

MARKET PRICES

The valuation problem of a commodity is greatly simplified if a market exists in which the commodity can be freely traded against money. Suppose, for example, that the price of rice is $2 per pound. A person's marginal willingness to pay for the first pound of rice consumed is, say, $10. Because their willingness to pay is greater than the price of the rice, this person will certainly purchase a first pound of rice, thereby generating a consumer surplus of $8. Because of the law of decreasing marginal utility, this person's marginal willingness to pay for a second pound of rice is less than $10; suppose it goes down to $5. Because the willingness to pay is still greater than the market price of the rice, it is optimal for this person to purchase a second pound of rice. In fact, this person will continue to purchase rice until their willingness to pay goes down to the market price of rice. All consumers would do the same, so that, at equilibrium, their marginal willingness to pay becomes $2. Thus, at equilibrium, the monetary value of rice will be the same for everyone, and will be equal to the price of rice.

Markets provide a strong machinery for value equalization. All people must value a good or service equally for an efficient allocation of resources in the economy. Indeed, if two people value a good differently, transferring one unit of the good from the person who values it less to the person who values it more would be mutually advantageous if the supplier were to obtain monetary compensation somewhere between the two individual valuations of the good. Suppose, for example, that person X values a pound of rice at $4, whereas person Y values it at $2. Then, transferring one pound of rice from Y to X against a price of $3 would increase the utility of the two agents.

If the market for rice is competitive, then the observed price of rice will also be equal to the marginal cost of producing rice. This is because profit-maximizing firms will find it profitable to increase their production as long as doing so increases their revenue more than their cost; that is, if the price of rice is greater than the marginal cost of rice. So, firms will produce more rice up to the point at which the marginal profit margin disappears; that is, when the marginal cost of producing rice equals the price of $2 per pound. All firms will do the same, so that all will face a marginal cost of rice of $2 per pound. This ensures that rice is produced at a minimum total cost in the economy. It is also an attractive property of competition that at equilibrium, the marginal cost of production is equal to the marginal value of the good, which is also equal to $2 per pound, as explained earlier. This implies that the total surplus associated with the market is maximized. Producing more units of a good would generate more cost than the monetary value that their consumption would generate. To illustrate, suppose that some technocrats believe that raising both the production and consumption of rice in a particular country would be socially desirable. Suppose, for example, they force rice producers to deliver more rice for state rice silos, to be distributed for free to the population. This additional production will cost more than $2 per ton because of diseconomies of scale. But because people value the additional consumption at less than $2 per ton, this action actually goes against the common good, as its net social benefit is negative.

These observations are of primary importance for cost–benefit analysis. Market prices are very useful indications of how people value goods and services, and of the collective costs associated with the production of goods and services. Evaluating the social impact of an action that modifies the allocation of market goods is therefore quite simple. For example, if a policy reduces the consumption of apples at the margin but increases the consumption of bananas, it is socially desirable if, and only if, the market value of the lost apples is less than the market value of the additional bananas. This means that one does not need to inquire about each individual preference when performing a cost-benefit analysis in this framework, since prices reveal them on markets. This greatly simplifies the work of the policy evaluators.

However, the conclusion that the market price of a good reveals both the social cost necessary to produce it and the utility benefit that it generates for those who consume it is correct only if conditions that I made implicitly in this section are satisfied. First, no participant in the market can have a "market power." In other words, all participants take the price as given. This condition is not satisfied, however, when the number of producers is small enough that they can push the price upward by coordinating a reduction in aggregate supply, as was done in 1973 by the Organization of the Petroleum Exporting Countries (OPEC) on the oil market. But other examples of anticompetitive behavior abound, and states have developed strong regulations to oppose them. Second, there can be no information asymmetry between parties about different aspects of the trade, such as the quality of the product. Finally, everyone must be able to observe the price at no cost and should be allowed to trade freely. These conditions are seldom satisfied perfectly, so one should remain prudent when using market prices to infer individual valuations. For example, the labor markets fail to satisfy these conditions. Regulations and syndicates—both of employers and of workers—limit competition. The freedom of parties to a labor contract is limited by various legal constraints, such as a minimum wage requirement. As a consequence, the equilibrium wage reveals neither the opportunity cost of leisure nor the marginal productivity of labor.

COMPETITION, VALUATION, AND FAIRNESS

I have just shown that, in the absence of friction, competition leads to an efficient allocation of production and consumption in the economy. In particular, it eliminates all mutually advantageous trades. But is the competitive equilibrium fair?

Efficiency and fairness are two different concepts. Economists have a unique definition of efficiency, which was introduced at the end of the nineteenth century by the Italian economist Vilfredo Pareto. An allocation of resources in the economy is considered "Pareto efficient" if there is no other feasible allocation in which all individuals are made better off. Implementing Pareto-efficient allocation would seem to be a desirable objective for society. Indeed, if a current allocation is not Pareto efficient, why not move to another allocation in which everyone is made better off? The first theorem of welfare economics states that in the absence of friction, the competitive equilibrium is Pareto efficient. It maximizes some *weighted* sum of individual well-beings.

The problem is that this notion of efficiency says nothing about how fair the allocation of these resources is. For example, giving all resources to Croesus may be Pareto efficient, since any transfer of some of these resources to other people would reduce the well-being of Croesus. If Croesus were to receive all resources as an initial endowment, it's easy to guess what the competitive equilibrium would be in this economy: Because nobody would have anything to sell except for Croesus, no trade would be possible, and the competitive equilibrium would have Croesus consuming everything. This competitive equilibrium is Pareto efficient, but it's clearly unfair.

Evaluating the degree of fairness of an allocation is difficult because there exists no consensual definition of fairness. For our purposes, I qualify an allocation as fair if it maximizes the *unweighted* sum of individual utilities. I defended this way of measuring social welfare in chapter 1. It is how an impartial and rational individual would evaluate social outcomes under the veil of ignorance.

Remember that in a competitive equilibrium, all consumers value one more apple in the same way. Remember also that individual monetary valuations are equal to the ratio of the marginal utilities of apples and income. Suppose first that there is no income inequality, so that all consumers have the same marginal utility of income. This implies that, at equilibrium, all consumers have the same marginal utility for apples. This means that departing from the competitive allocation of that commodity through a feasible reallocation would have no effect on the unweighted sum of individual utility at the margin. In this sense, the competitive allocation of apples is fair. Under the veil of ignorance with regard to who is who, people would be glad to promote competition as a fair and efficient way to allocate resources in the economy.

Suppose, alternatively, that the distribution of income in the economy is unequal. Wealthy people have a smaller marginal utility of income than those who are poor, and similarly a smaller marginal utility for apples, too. Thus, the ratio of the two, which is the willingness to pay for apples, equals the market price of apples at equilibrium. The important thing to keep in mind here is that wealthy people have a smaller marginal utility for everything; in this case, apples and bananas. Therefore, redistributing apples from the wealthy to the poor necessarily increases the unweighted sum of individual well-beings. This shows that the competitive equilibrium is unfair. In fact, the competitive equilibrium maximizes a weighted sum of individual utility, where the individual weights are equal to the inverse of their marginal utility of income. In other words, the competitive equilibrium is supported by a social welfare function in which wealthy people get a larger weight than those who are not wealthy. The competitive equilibrium is only one example of a Pareto-efficient allocation. It puts more weight on the well-being of those who are better off in the social welfare that is maximized. Redistributing resources from the wealthy to the poor increases the sum of individual utilities, but to the detriment of the wealthy.

Thus, even if markets work perfectly, we can easily envision a redistributive role for public intervention and social activism. The case for this is particularly striking when evaluating actions aimed at promoting the development of poor countries. For example, in the case of the Rana Plaza scandal, the unsafe working conditions and low salaries of Bangladesh may be the outcome of competition, which is good for economic efficiency. But at the same time, such conditions are a very unsatisfactory outcome in terms of fairness. A typical difficulty here is to improve fairness without destroying efficiency. For example, a standard redistribution tool is income taxation. But income taxation tends to reduce the incentive to work, and to incentivize the most productive people to migrate toward fiscal havens. Therefore, it has an adverse effect on the creation of value generated by working that could be redistributed. I will come back to this issue later on in the chapter when I discuss the Laffer curve.

EXTERNALITIES AND PUBLIC GOODS

Competitive markets are not only unfair in general, they can also be very bad in demonstrating social values. In a market economy, since people actually pay for the goods they consume, they reveal their preferences through their consumption decisions. All people who purchase rice at $2 per pound reveal that their valuation of this good is at least equal to this price, and is in fact equal to it for the last pound of rice purchased. This price also signals to all market participants the social cost associated with the production of this product and induces them to internalize this social value in their decision to consume it.

The invisible hand does not always work well. Markets fail to allocate resources in line with the common good. The best example of market failure comes from the existence of externalities. An externality is generated each time an agent's action has an impact on the well-being of another agent in the absence of any contractual arrangement between the two parties. Pollution is a classic externality. When I drive in the city, my car emits microparticulates that harm the health of city dwellers. I don't have to pay for "consuming" the city's clean air—even through the city's inhabitants place a high value on it. But since I don't have to pay a price to "consume" clean air, I consume too much of it. In plain English, people pollute too much. According to a recent Massachusetts Institute of Technology study (Caiazzo et al., 2013), around two hundred thousand early deaths occur in the United States each year owing to combustion emissions, with road transportation and energy generation being the main contributors. Such negative externalities are everywhere. They contribute to global warming, the deterioration of bio-diversity, and pollution that reduces life expectancy and the quality of many environmental assets that future generations will inherit.

Drèze and Gollier (1993) and Blanchard and Tirole (2008) remind us that, from the viewpoint of firms, the lay-off of an employee is optimal as soon as the marginal pro-ductivity of their labor is less than their gross wage. In the context of massive involuntary unemployment, employers do not take into account the unemployment benefits paid by the state to unemployed workers. In other words, firms do not internalize this negative externality when determin-ing their employment levels in recession, which implies an excess of layoffs. In a closed economy, this may justify levying layoff taxes to induce firms to internalize the social cost of unemployment. When employers contribute to the funding of unemployment insurance, a bonus-malus system should be put in place in which firms that intensively use temporary layoffs should contribute more to the system.

Not all externalities are negative, however. There are also positive externalities; that is, actions that others benefit from without having to pay for. Knowledge externalities are a good example: new knowledge generated by research activi-ties in universities and by corporate R&D benefit society as a whole. Only a fraction of this knowledge is actually pro-tected by patents. But even though such knowledge is a posi-tive externality, the fact that one gets this knowledge for free sends a bad signal to innovators, who may not invest enough in research as a consequence. Vaccination is another example of a positive externality, since one's vaccination reduces the probability that someone else will become ill. But again, the fact that another person can get this protection for free induces people to underestimate the social value of their decision to get vaccinated. A third example of positive externality can be found on the labor market. Hiring more people in a firm generates a private benefit for the firm, which is the additional revenue generated by the increased output net of the additional labor cost. However, the effort exerted by new hires is not an externality, because they are covered by a labor contract and a wage that compensates them for it. But hiring more people also reduces the financial burden of the public unemployment insurance scheme, and this positive externality is usually not taken into account by employers. The other side of the coin is the negative externality generated by laying off more people in economic downturns. Moreover, employing people increases their human capital, which is good for the employer only if these employees stay with the firm in the long run. In reality, since slavery has been abolished, employers' investments in their employees' human capital are an externality that benefits other employers.

Social interactions offer other examples of positive externalities. For example, the time that my wife and I spent educating our children to behave prosocially does not benefit just our children. It also benefits their friends, through both their generosity and the exemplarity of their behavior. A good attitude is mimetic. Also, helping our children with their homework helps them learn more, and this is good for the other children in their classrooms. Indeed, one of the well-known determinants of a child's success in school is the general level of culture and intelligence of their friends. All these examples illustrate the production of externalities that are not internalized by people through a price mechanism.

There are also externalities associated with the process of consuming goods and services. Driving a Rolls-Royce may be good for the well-being of the driver, but it may generate envy in other people on the road. Conspicuous goods are often consumed precisely because they demonstrate the social prestige of their owners. The existence of these status goods may be a negative-sum game. I always fly economy because it is clear to me that the private benefit of flying business class is at least two orders of magnitude smaller than the cost of a business-class ticket for my employer. It's also because business-class passengers exert a negative externality on others. More traditional examples of consumption externalities are traffic congestion and pollution.

The existence of public goods is another source of market inefficiency. Public goods are goods whose consumption by an agent does not prohibit other agents from also consuming them, and for which it is difficult to exclude some people from consuming them. Most types of public infrastructure (e.g., roads, national parks, the Internet) and services (e.g., education, research, homeland security) are examples of public goods. Because of the property of nonexcludability of public goods, it is not usually possible to ask consumers to pay for what they consume, so markets do not work well to produce the public goods that are valuable to consumers. Most consumers will prefer to "free-ride" by expecting to benefit from the production of public goods that others would finance. Therefore, at equilibrium, in the absence of external public intervention, there will be an under-provision of these goods. When states were weak, as in the Middle Ages in Europe, roads, bridges, schools, and hospitals were in bad shape, if they existed at all. Fire protection and garbage collection were nonexistent even in large cities, as is still the case today in many developing countries. Everyone would benefit from producing more public goods, but nobody wants to contribute to their financing. People value these goods, but they opportunistically refuse to pay for it. The emergence of stronger and more responsible—that is, more democratic—states helped improve the situation by forcing citizens to contribute to the funding of these public goods through the tax system.

In the case of both externalities and public goods, markets don't provide the right signals about societal values. This raises two questions. First, how can we restore efficiency? Second, how should we measure values? In the case of externalities, the first question is quite simple to answer. Everyone has heard about the "polluter pays" principle, which states that if someone exerts a negative externality on someone else, the former should compensate the latter at a level corresponding to the monetary damage. In addition to its own appeal in terms of justice, this principle restores economic efficiency by forcing people to internalize the damages that one's action imposes on others. This can be done, for example, by taxing polluting activities, with the tax attached to an activity equaling the marginal damage that it generates in the economy. A system of tradable permits for pollution would have the same effect, if the equilibrium price of the permits equaled the marginal damage of the pollution. In the employment example provided earlier, the negative externality associated with layoffs may justify taxing them.

This pollution-pay principle has a positive aspect when applied to a positive externality, as in the case of prosocial behaviors or actions favorable to the quality of the environment (e.g., recycling, gardening). A person who exerts a positive externality on others should be compensated for that, at the level of social value generated. But as explained by Benabou and Tirole (2006), for example, altruistic people may value their own production of positive externalities and public goods because it improves their self-image and reputation as a good person. However, this is possible only if the activity entails a sacrifice for the person. On the contrary, the existence of a monetary reward can annihilate the positive image associated with these good deeds and can therefore reduce the willingness to produce positive externalities and public goods. This is why blood donations are often made without compensation, for example. Similarly, the negative stigma of antisocial behaviors such as polluting can be sufficient to deter people from taking part in them owing to concern for their self-esteem and reputation. However, the existence of a tax system or permit-to-pollute system may suppress such a deterrent effect by eliminating the stigma. The intrinsic motivation to appear to be a good person would then be crowded out by the extrinsic motivation of the monetary incentive scheme. Globally, this incentive scheme could actually be counterproductive.

HEDONIC VALUATION

This brings us to the second question: how to measure value. The price signal conveyed by taxing a polluter should be equal to the marginal damage generated by the pollution. Some of the impacts of the pollution could have a direct monetary impact on victims, such as lost labor income owing to pollution-induced illness, but other impacts may be nonmonetary. Pollution reduces the quality of the environment and adversely affects the health of the population. To restore efficiency, the price signal should equal the monetized utility loss incurred by the victims in order to induce the polluter to fully internalize the social consequences of their actions. It is thus crucial to measure the social value of such damages with precision. In the absence of the consent of the victims, it is not possible to use revealed preferences to measure this directly from the observation of market prices and individual decisions.

However, the technique of "hedonic valuation" can often provide an indirect method of measuring social value. Consider a city in which all houses are identical except for some, which are more exposed to the pollution produced by a nearby factory than others. If the real estate market is efficient and the information about the pollution concentration in different areas is made public, then differences in house prices should reflect how much people value the quality of their environment. Of course, in reality not all houses are identical, and many other parameters—some correlated with pollution—influence house prices. But standard econometric tools can be used to isolate the effect of pollution on these prices. Thus, although pollution is not directly priced in markets, the price of certain goods—here, real estate assets—can help us infer how people value other goods—here, the quality of their environment.

It often happens that, as in the Rana Plaza case, private and collective actions generate health externalities; that is, such actions affect life expectancy, mortality risk, and morbidity. In order to evaluate such an action, we need to value lives. In the 1950s, economists developed the concept of the value of statistical life to evaluate policies associated with health externalities. It is defined as the cost a group is willing to pay to prevent one death . It can also be defined as an individual's marginal willingness to pay to marginally reduce their risk of death. For example, if a person is willing to pay $100 to reduce a mortality risk by 1 in 100,000, their value of statistical life is $10 million.

One can use a hedonic valuation technique to value lives. As documented by Davis (2004), an isolated county in Nevada experienced a severe surge of pediatric leukemia cases between 1998 and 2002, with the estimated lifetime pediatric leukemia risk per ten thousand individuals rising from 2.6 to 14.5 during this period. The probability of observing this surge by pure chance was almost zero, so people started to hypothesize that it was linked to an unknown local pollutant. Fewer people now wanted to live in the area, which led to a reduction in the price of houses. House prices continued to drop until people saw an advantage to living in there: the lower price of houses perfectly compensating for the perceived increased risk of dying from pediatric leukemia. Davis (2004) obtained estimates that "indicate that houses sold during the period of maximum risk sold for 15.6 percent less than equivalent houses not affected by the leukemia increase." This estimation led to a value of statistical life of around $5.5 million for people living in the county in 2002.

In other hedonic valuation studies, differences in wages are compared to the mortality risks of the corresponding jobs and generate similar value of statistical life estimations. As documented by Cropper, Hammitt, and Robinson (2011), current estimates of the value of statistical life in the United States are somewhere around $6 million. This means that it is socially desirable to implement any action that costs less than that amount per statistical life saved. In France, the value of statistical life used in public policy evaluations is $2 million.

Different countries use different values of statistical life to perform cost–benefit analyses. This is in part due to the fact that the value per statistical life is expected to evolve with income. The crude reality is that life and health are typically worth less in poor countries than in rich ones, as suggested by the Rana Plaza catastrophe in Bangladesh. There are routine medical treatments in rich countries that cost hundreds of thousands of dollars; these are simply not available to the citizens of poor countries. The hard reality is that many Bangladeshis face more immediate priorities than improving their health or reducing their risk of fatal accidents—such as addressing the more immediate risk of starvation. Given the lower value of life in this country, other public strategies, such as investing in education or road infrastructure, for example, could well have a better impact on social welfare than improving safety in the workplace. Based on international comparisons and a meta-analysis of the literature on the hedonic valuation of the value of statistical life, Hammitt and Robinson (2011) suggest that a 1 percent reduction in income reduces the VSL by 1 percent. In economics jargon, this means that the value of statistical life has an income elasticity equaling 1.

So, if the income per capita in the United States is approximately fifty times greater than in Bangladesh (which is around $1,100), the implication is that a value of statistical life of $6 million in the United States corresponds to a VSL of roughly $120,000 in Bangladesh. In other words, one would be fifty times less willing to save a life in Bangladesh than in the United States. This is another illustration that although the competitive equilibrium may be efficient, it is generally not fair.

COST-BENEFIT ANALYSIS

Measuring individual values is the first crucial step to any evaluation of collective actions. These actions often entail heterogeneous consequences for different stakeholders. In the Rana Plaza case, for example, improving workplace safety standards in Bangladesh would reduce the mortality risk of jobs, but it would also increase the unemployment rate and increase the price of clothing around the world. An improved safety policy would thus generate winners and losers, with gains and losses that are different in nature. To determine whether such a policy would be socially desirable, economists us the so-called Kaldor–Hicks compensation criterion, which states that an allocation A is preferred to allocation B if everybody is at least as happy with A as they are with B after monetary transfers between winners and losers (which may or may not occur).What this criterion does in reality is test whether a policy increases social welfare by using individual weights in the aggregation of individual well-beings corresponding to those that support a competitive equilibrium.

Consider, for example, a firm that pollutes the water of a river used by the inhabitants of a nearby city. The state contemplates the possibility of forcing the firm to reduce its emissions of the pollutant through a new environmental norm. The clear loser of the policy would be the firm and its stakeholders: its shareholders; its employees, who could lose their jobs because of the reduced competitiveness of the firm; and potentially its customers, who could have to pay a higher price for its product. The clear winners would be the population living in the city who will drink healthier water. The Kaldor–Hicks compensation criterion tells us that the new policy would be desirable if the sum of what the city's inhabitants would be willing to pay for the better water is high enough to compensate the stakeholders of the firm for their loss. The hedonic valuation technique can be used to estimate the city dwellers' willingness to pay. Whether the compensation of the losers by the winners actually occurs is irrelevant for this efficiency test. This is a pure efficiency criterion, with no concern for fairness.

Take another example: In mid-November 2015, Brussels was all but shut down for five days because of a deadly terrorist attack. In doing this, Belgian authorities probably saved lives, but at the same time, hundreds of millions of euros were lost because of the closure of shops, companies, schools, and other public institutions. The Kaldor–Hicks compensation criterion raises the question of whether the value of the reduced risk of death as a result of terrorism for the people living in Brussels was greater than the income loss. Suppose the safety policy was expected to save one hundred lives. If the Belgian value of statistical life was $2 million, then the policy would be desirable only if the income lost was less than $200 million.

When an action passes the Kaldor–Hicks compensation test, the benefit of the winner is large enough to compensate the loss of the losers. In other words, such an action, accompanied by some transfer from the winners to the losers can make everyone better off. However, most often these transfers are not implemented, which implies that some efficient actions are resisted by the uncompensated losers. The "not in my back yard" (NIMBY) effect illustrates this fact. For example, the Toulouse airport is so close to the city that many people incur its many externalities (e.g., noise, pollution, congestion). Twenty years ago, city officials wanted to move the airport to a less dense area close to where I live. This action would certainly have passed the Kaldor–Hicks test, but it has never been implemented because the residents of my neighborhood believed—probably correctly—that they would never be compensated for the airport's many negative externalities. Globalization is another example of a situation where benefits vastly dominate costs but where losers are not compensated. Immigration is also likely to pass the Kaldor–Hicks test, but it also fails to induce winners to compensate losers to make it a win–win situation. Migrants clearly contribute to economic growth in the host country. But it is also often suggested that low-skilled workers suffer from the arrival of new migrants, although this is still a very controversial question among labor economists. The absence of compensation is a catastrophic political failure that may be conducive to populism. But in fact, the main source of stagnation of the low-skilled wages in the Western world may well come from competition with robots, which raises another set of problems.

Cost–benefit analysis is the operational version of the Kaldor–Hicks compensation criterion. It generalizes a simple decision rule to the collective level. At the individual level, it is optimal to invest more in safety if the individual marginal willingness to pay for safety is greater than its cost. At the collective level, it is socially desirable to improve safety if the marginal willingness to pay for safety aggregated among all individuals in a group is greater than the cost. If this is the case, the action will pass the Kaldor–Hicks test, for example by considering monetary transfers in which everyone pays an amount equal to their marginal willingness to pay for safety. This would leave everyone with the same level of well-being, and it would yield a profit for the institution in charge of the reform. More generally, the cost–benefit analysis technique consists of comparing the social benefit of an action with its social cost. If the social benefit is larger than the social cost, a reform passes the Kaldor–Hicks test and the reform is socially desirable. Costs and benefits are all measured in monetary terms by summing the marginal willingness to pay of the different stakeholders affected by the action.

Because the value of statistical life is smaller in poor countries, standard cost–benefit analysis supports actions aimed at transferring unsafe activities to these countries. Although doing so increases the mortality risk in these countries, the amounts that rich countries are willing to pay are much larger than what is necessary to compensate for the additional risk. This makes everyone better off. For example, poor countries are able to spend the additional revenue on education, hospitals, and transportation infrastructure, all of which are critically important for development. Because poor people also tend to value their environment less, this suggests that poor countries should not only be less safe, but also more polluted. This point is linked to a well-known controversy associated to a leaked (ironic?) memo written by former U.S. Treasury Secretary Larry Summers in 1991, when he was at the World Bank, suggesting that dirty industries should be transferred to less developed countries.

It's easy to argue that these kinds of measures are heartless, or to invoke the World Bank or Larry Summers as scapegoats. But the truth is that the competitive pressure for cheaper garments comes from our own consumption behavior. This pressure brings Bangladeshis' income down, which lowers their own willingness to pay for safety. Consciously or not, these values factor into the cost–benefit analysis performed by selfish agents, such as consumers in garment stores ("Should I pay $40 for a locally manufactured T-shirt or $10 for one made in Bangladesh?") and entrepreneurs when determining the location of a new garment production plant ("Should I build in the United States and pay wages of $10 an hour or in Bangladesh where I can pay a fraction of that?"). These cost–benefit valuations are hard to condemn in a competitive world. If all clothing companies around the world were to locate their production in Bangladesh, it would be difficult for any specific company to deviate, as they would face the risk of losing customers. For example, a garment producer who unilaterally decides to raise wages and safety norms above the sector standard faces the risk of being wiped out of the market if not enough consumer activists are willing to pay more for the clothing they produce. This would be a self-defeating strategy. As Larry Summers once said, "You can't repeal the laws of economics. Even if they are inconvenient."

Most readers will find this message uncomfortable, as I do. But such recommendations are simply the consequences of a much deeper, undesirable characteristic of our world. The real scandal is the incredible level of income inequality existing on this planet. The cost–benefit analysis toolbox can and should also be used to value the reduction of these inequalities, as I'll show now. This discussion provides a solution to the Summers's "dirty industries controversy" and to the Rana Plaza scandal for public institutions and activists who are not willing to accept the highly unfair implicit weights of the utilitarian social welfare function that supports the competitive equilibrium.

DISTRIBUTIVE JUSTICE AND THE VALUATION OF INEQUALITIES

Because the marginal utility of income decreases as income increases, transferring income from the wealthy to the poor increases the sum of individual utility. This transfer is often referred to as a Pigou–Dalton transfer and has the characteristic of reducing inequality. One dollar more of income for the poor has the potential to save a life, whereas one dollar more for the wealthy has a much smaller impact on an individual's well-being. This explains why a Pigou–Dalton transfer increases unweighted social welfare. This result is driven by the fact that wealthy people value one dollar more of income less than do those who are poor. Technically, this means that utility is increasing and concave in income, implying a decreasing marginal utility of income. When individual income rises, individual utility also rises but faster at lower income levels than at higher ones. This implies that under the veil of ignorance, all individuals would be in favor of reducing inequality through a Pigou–Dalton transfer, as doing so would raise expected utility. To illustrate, consider a community of two people, one poor and one wealthy. Suppose that the poor person would see their utility increased by 1 if they could get one dollar more of income, whereas for wealthy person, the utility gain would be only 0.1. Then, transferring one dollar of income from the wealthy person to the poor person would increase the sum of utility by 0.9, or the expected utility by half this value. Thus, an impartial and rational individual, under the veil of ignorance, should be in favor of this reduction of inequalities, as explained by

Atkinson (1970). The benefit of the reduced inequality is increasing in the speed at which marginal utility goes down when income increases. This implies that any cost–benefit analysis should include a measurement of the welfare benefit generated by the reduction in inequality generated by the action under scrutiny.

It is useful to estimate our collective degree of inequality aversion. Suppose that we live in a society with two social classes of the same size. Suppose also that the upper class is twice as rich as the lower class. Imagine a leaky Pigou–Dalton policy of income transfer from rich to poor with deadweight losses, in the sense that from one dollar collected from the rich, only twenty-five cents can be redistributed to the poor, the other seventy-five cents being lost to all. Do you think this is a desirable policy? There are both a benefit and a cost associated with this policy. The benefit is the socially desirable reduction in inequality, and the cost is the reduction in the aggregate income by seventy-five cents. So, the question can be rephrased in terms of whether you value the reduction of inequality at more than seventy-five cents. This depends upon your degree of inequality aversion.

Suppose that the income elasticity of marginal utility is −1; that is, that a 1 percent increase in income reduces marginal utility by 1 percent. In this case, we would say that the intensity of inequality aversion equals 1. Because, in our example, the rich have an income twice that of the poor, the marginal utility of the rich is 50 percent smaller than the marginal utility of the poor. Thus, the impact of the one-dollar reduction in income for the poor has an effect on the utility of the rich equivalent to a fifty-cent reduction in income for the poor. Because the poor only receive twenty-five cents, this is not enough to compensate the rich. The policy thus fails to pass the Kaldor–Hicks compensation test, and the policy should be rejected. But this evaluation depends heavily upon the assumption that the income elasticity of marginal utility equals −1. If marginal utility were to decrease faster with income, the impartial evaluator would be more inequality averse and should place more value on the proposed reduction in inequality. Suppose, for example, that the income elasticity of marginal utility is −2. Here, we would say that the intensity of inequality aversion equals 2. Then, the one-dollar reduction in income for the rich would have an impact on utility equivalent to a reduction of income for the poor by twenty-five cents. This implies that the twenty-five-cent transfer to the poor is just enough to compensate the rich. Thus, if inequality aversion equals 2, one should be simply indifferent as to whether to implement the policy.

A central problem is to determine the degree of inequality aversion that represents our collective moral attitude. The Greek letter γ is often used to represent the degree of inequality aversion. Suppose that for each dollar taken from the rich, only $1 - c$ dollar goes to the poor, and c is lost to all. In your opinion, what is the maximum loss c per dollar collected from the rich that one should be willing to accept? If you have no sensitivity to inequality, inequality is zero by definition, and the answer should be 0. If a group's collective preferences entail some inequality aversion, you can tolerate some positive deadweight loss to redistribute.

Table 2.1 Maximum Acceptable Loss per Dollar Collected from the Upper Class (Two Times Richer) as a Function of the Inequality Aversion Index

Inequality Aversion	Maximum Loss per Dollar Collected
0	0.00
0.5	0.29
1	0.50
1.5	0.65
2	0.75
4	0.94
10	0.999

In table 2.1, I calculate the link between this maximum loss and the inequality aversion index. If we all agree that, in this context, it is reasonable to assume the maximum loss should be somewhere between fifty and seventy-five cents, one should use an inequality aversion index of somewhere between 1 and 2.

Under the veil of ignorance, aversion to inequality can be interpreted as risk aversion. Suppose that, in limbo, one flips a coin to determine the social class to which one belongs. In this case, the issue of redistribution raised earlier can be interpreted as a form of insurance to reduce the risk of being born poor. If the poor are less poor and the rich less rich, people in limbo will perceive less risk about their future social status. Risk aversion is a much easier concept to estimate than inequality aversion because it is linked to individual preferences rather than to ethical attitudes. Measures of risk aversion have been created by using observed behavior in financial and insurance decisions. For example, Drèze (1981) suggests that an inequality aversion index of around 4 could explain the choice of insurance deductibles by households. As we will see later on, the so-called equity premium puzzle suggests an even larger intensity of risk aversion. It is not rare to read papers on macroeconomics and finance theory using an inequality aversion index of around 10.

The typical lab experiment performed to estimate the individual intensity of risk aversion typically goes as follows. You are offered two heads-or-tails gambles. In gamble A, you have an equal chance of getting either $50 or $100. In gamble B, you have an equal chance of getting either $50.50 or $99. Observe that this is exactly the choice with which people in limbo were confronted when evaluating the policy consisting of the leaky Pigou–Dalton transfer examined earlier, with an initial income of $50 or $100 for the poor and rich, respectively. This reinforces the idea that inequality is risk under the veil of ignorance, and that inequality aversion is risk aversion.

The main instrument used to reduce income inequalities is the income tax system. It is thus natural to examine our national tax rules to infer our collective aversion to inequality. Suppose that the progressivity of the tax system is based on the principle of equal absolute sacrifice of satisfaction. This means that all citizens are taxed such that the absolute utility cost of their income tax is the same. Because marginal utility is decreasing, wealthy people should pay more tax under this principle. By how much they actually do tells us something about the speed at which marginal utility decreases with income. For example, if inequality aversion is 2, this would mean that doubling incomes should quadruple income taxation. Evans and Sezer (2005) inferred from this approach that the inequality aversion index was between 1.4 and 1.6 for fifteen of the twenty-seven members of the European Union. More recently, Groom and Maddison (2016) estimated $\gamma \approx 1.5$ by examining the U.K. income tax system. However, this approach was based on at least two unrealistic assumptions. First, it overlooked the fact that high marginal income tax reduces willingness to work, a source of moral hazard. This yields the famous Laffer curve. Most lawmakers understand that taxing income may induce taxpayers to work less or to migrate to tax havens. This tends to limit the progressivity of the income tax system, so that the observed progressivity does not fully reveal our collective attitude toward inequality. The opportunistic behavior of taxpayers limits our collective ability to tax incomes. Second, the political equilibrium offers no guarantee that the income tax system will be socially efficient. In other words, the majority system is unlikely to generate an optimal tax schedule.

Various approaches have been used to estimate the elasticity of marginal utility γ, and the jury is still out on which is best. In an intertemporal context, Stern (1977) obtained a best estimate of inequality aversion of around 2 in a relatively wide confidence interval of between 0 and 10. Hall (1988) proposed an inequality aversion of around 10, whereas Epstein and Zin (1991) arrived at a value of between 1.25 and 5. Further, Pearce and Ulph (1995) have suggested an inequality aversion of between 0.7 and 1.5. Other recommendations in the literature about the choice of inequality

Table 2.2 Expert Recommendations for the Inequality Aversion Index

Author (Year)	Inequality Aversion, γ
Stern (1977)	2
Cline (1992)	1.5
Intergovernmental Panel on Climate Change (1995)	1.5–2
Arrow (1999)	2
HM Treasury (2003)	1
Lebègue (2005)	2
Arrow (2007)	2–3
Stern (2007)	1
Weitzman (2007b)	2
Dasgupta (2008)	2–4
Nordhaus (2008)	2
Pindyck (2013)	1–3

aversion index are summarized in table 2.2. Following Stern (1977), IPCC (1995), Arrow (2007), Weitzman (2007a), Nordhaus (2008), and Pindyck (2013), I will use an inequality aversion index of $\gamma = 2$.

Let me now extrapolate this approach to an international analysis. If we agree that our collective degree of inequality aversion is around 2, then one should be willing to sacrifice as much as \$2,500 to give \$1 to Bangladeshis who are fifty times poorer than us. But we don't do that in the real world. We don't help Bangladeshis very much to improve the safety of their garment factories. We don't help them improve their health, education, or transportation infrastructure. This is because competition leads to great international inequality, which in turn leads to extreme levels of heterogeneity in our valuation of lives. Competition maybe efficient, but it is not fair. Price signals may be useful for exploiting trade gains, but these price signals may not represent our societal values.

It can be interesting to estimate the social cost of inequality in the world. Suppose one could completely eliminate world inequality as it is today by moving to an egalitarian world. If inequality aversion equals 2, what is the minimum egalitarian income in this alternative world that would make the move ethically desirable? A simple answer is that, with an inequality aversion of 2, one should be willing to move to an egalitarian world if the income there is at least equal to 37 percent of the current world's per capita gross domestic product (GDP).[1] This confirms the importance that inequality reduction should have in any cost–benefit analysis evaluating public policies or prosocial actions. Reducing income inequality has a high social value.

The aversion to inequality that I described earlier with the utilitarian approach is reinforced when utilitarianism is replaced by prioritarianism. As explained in chapter 1, prioritarianism implies putting more weight on the utility of less well-off people. This obviously reinforces the positive impact that a Pigou–Dalton transfer would have on the social welfare function. The extreme Rawlsian version of prioritarianism is to put no collective value on any increase in utility of any other person than the poorest one. Within this framework, our collective aversion to inequality of consumption has two origins: an individually rational one and a moral one. Under the veil of ignorance, it is rational to dislike inequality because of the decreasing marginal utility of income, as explained earlier. The moral argument is specific to prioritarianism: Because of the focus on the utility of the poorest, increasing the income of the poor has an additional social benefit.

Until now, I have limited my analysis to the measurement of income inequality aversion. But unweighted utilitarian welfare also entails aversion to inequalities in the other determinants of individual well-being; for example, consumption of specific goods and services, life expectancy, and the quality of the environment. For example, people prefer to live longer, but it is believed that the marginal utility of a longer life is decreasing. Thus, because Bangladeshis live shorter lives than Americans, transferring years of life from the United States to Bangladesh would be socially desirable; that is, it would raise the unweighted sum of well-beings in the world. The degree of aversion to inequality in life expectancy need not be identical to income inequality aversion.

But there is a fundamental dilemma in using this approach in cost–benefit analysis, as it implies a form of paternalism. The standard cost–benefit analysis approach based on the Kaldor–Hicks compensation test takes individual valuations as what they are given the actual allocation of resources in the economy. These valuations are compatible with the maximization of a weighted sum of individual utilities, where wealthier people are better represented. Valuations compatible with the maximization of an unweighted sum of individual utilities are different. For example, it would typically generate a value of statistical life in poor countries that is greater than what poor people are willing to pay to reduce their own mortality risk. Using these valuations would be wasteful and paternalistic. If altruistic people in the West put a value of statistical life of $2 million in Bangladesh, but Bangladeshis valued life at only $100,000, the West would find many actions that save lives in the country socially desirable that Bangladeshis would find undesirable if they were to use their own money to fund them. A better idea would then be for altruistic Westerners to make a donation to Bangladesh for an equivalent amount and let the country decide what to do with the money. A nonpaternalistic compromise in cost–benefit analysis would therefore consist of using individual valuations of nonmonetary determinants of well-being as what they are, while at the same time valuing the reduction of income inequalities as described earlier. Fleurbaey and Zuber (2017) offer an interesting critical discussion about how to combine fainess and social risk management.

A ROLE FOR SOCIALLY RESPONSIBLE INVESTORS

This chapter delivers a relatively simple message to socially responsible investors; that is, those investors who take account of the extra-financial (social and environmental) performance of their investments. If competitive markets were efficient and fair, profit would be the correct measure of the creation of social value generated by the activities of a firm. Indeed, profit would be the measure of the difference between social benefits and social costs—the difference between customers' marginal willingness to pay and the social opportunity cost of inputs. For example, the rice producers we examined earlier cannot do anything else to create social value than to produce up to the point where the marginal cost of rice equals $2 per pound. This marginal cost represents the cost incurred by society as a whole to produce this good: the social cost of the workers' effort, the opportunity cost of using land for rice rather than other crops, the cost of capital, and so on. Because $2 per pound also represents the social value extracted by the consumers of the rice, there is no way to create more net social benefit than what is obtained by the profit-maximizing solution. This value creation is shared by the participants of the market: the profit for the owner of the firm, a consumer surplus for those with a willingness to pay for rice of more than $2 per pound, and a worker surplus for workers whose reservation wage is below the actual wage in the sector.

As explained earlier, this competitive allocation has at least two problems. First, the sharing of the social surplus need not to be fair, and in general it is not. Second, it is often the case that the price of the product does not entirely reflect the true value of its consumption and the social costs that its production necessitates, because of the existence of positive and negative externalities generated in the production and consumption process. So, the competitive allocation is neither efficient nor fair. Could responsible investors do something about that?

Competitive firms are not in a position to behave in a way that is compatible with a fair social welfare objective. This means that profit is an imperfect measure of a firm's creation of social value. For example, firms that have a smaller environmental footprint than their competitors may generate a smaller profit but create greater social value when one takes environmental performance into account. Other positive and negative externalities generated by firms should also be taken into account to measure their extra-financial performance, such as their contribution to the production of nonappropriable new knowledge or to the reduction of inequalities around the world.

Socially responsible investment funds have usually proceeded by eliminating firms they consider environmentally or socially irresponsible from their portfolio. This strategy is simple to implement if the extra-financial criteria used by these funds are easy to estimate, but it can overshoot a fund's social objective. A better way forward, going back to the utilitarian foundation presented earlier, would be to measure the contribution of each productive activity to social welfare by replacing profit with a new measure of social performance that combines profit with the monetized value of the extra-financial performance of each firm.

For example, if a firm emits greenhouse gases without being penalized for it, from the point of view of a socially responsible investor, its profit should be reduced by the marginal damage generated by these emissions. By fixing a value to carbon dioxide emissions (hopefully equaling the marginal damage they generate), the socially responsible investment fund would be able to re-estimate the true social performance of firms and use this in the optimal portfolio allocation in such funds. So, if a firm generated $2 of revenue over a certain period of time for each dollar invested, together with twenty kilograms of carbon dioxide emissions, its social benefit would be only $1.20 per dollar invested if carbon dioxide emissions are valued at $40 per ton. If another firm with the same risk profile yielded $1.80 per dollar invested but produced only ten kilograms of carbon dioxide emissions, it should be recognized as creating more social value.

One could use the same strategy for all kinds of social benefits. The value generated by reducing inequalities or improving workplace safety could be included in the process by using a transparent way to value both life and the reduction of inequalities. If this net value creation is spread over many periods and is uncertain, discounting and portfolio diversification should be used.

What is the impact of socially responsible investors and social responsible investment funds on the economy? If their share in the supply of capital is large enough, they will tend to reduce the cost of capital of virtuous firms and increase it for irresponsible ones. The disinvestment of socially responsible investors would have a result similar to that of imposing a carbon tax. But rather than having to pay the tax, firms would have to incur an equivalent increase in their cost of capital. Just as with a tax, this increase in cost of capital would induce firms to internalize their extra-financial performance in the evaluation of their own strategies, as explained by Gollier and Pouget (2015). To be frank, the approach of addressing climate change through socially responsible investing and cost of capital is limited by the fact that most investors are not socially responsible, in the sense that they are interested only in the financial performance of their portfolio. For such investors, the reduced price of brown and vice stocks that socially responsible investors orchestrate offers a windfall to investors who don't focus on socially responsible investments. A lower price means a larger return. This implies that investors who don't focus on socially responsible investments will at least partially undo the efforts of socially responsible investors by increasing the demand for brown and vice stocks, thereby reducing the cost of capital that socially responsible investors had originally increased through their more responsible portfolio choices.

Because socially responsible investment funds are interested in the extra-financial performance of the assets in which they invest, common wisdom suggests that they should financially underperform more traditional funds that aim to maximize the risk-adjusted financial return of their portfolios. This isn't necessarily true. For example, if green public policies that penalize firms for greenhouse gas emissions are implemented, heavy emitters will be negatively affected, implying that socially responsible investment funds will financially outperform traditional funds. If, in addition, we believe that this "carbon risk" is currently not priced, there is no cost associated with penalizing carbon-intensive firms by socially responsible investment in the business-as-usual scenario. This idea has recently been developed by Andersson, Bolton, and Samama (2015).

Have investors divested from carbon-intensive firms in the recent past? Such divestment would be desirable for socially responsible investors, and optimal for investors who don't focus on socially responsible investments and believe that one day, a coherent international carbon policy will emerge that will penalize carbon-intensive firms. If that were to happen some time in the future, many fossil fuel assets would become stranded. For example, a builder of a new coal power plant in Europe today faces the risk that it will become obsolete when such a policy materializes, with the asset becoming stranded. The anticipation of this scenario happening in ten or twenty years would induce investors to divest early enough, possibly today, to escape the future capital loss. For example, highly valued oil reserves would see their market capitalization dramatically depressed if investors were to start to believe that most of the oil in those reserves will never be burned. But divesting from fossil fuel assets would be optimal for purely financially motivated investors only if they were to believe in the emergence of a coherent and punitive international carbon policy in the future.

Some commentators have claimed that this is, in fact, already happening. Their claim is supported by the fact that several coal firms in the United States have recently gone under, in particular Peabody Energy, which went bankrupt in April 2016. However, the simpler explanation in this case is that the coal industry in the United States has been killed by the fast-growing shale gas industry and by the low price of oil in international markets. This explanation is supported by the wave of divestment announcements by many universities and pension and sovereign funds over the last few years. This divestment wave should depress the price of carbon-intensive assets on financial markets, and it should symmetrically raise the price of low-carbon assets. An investor who entered early enough in this movement should earn a fortune. But did this really happen? Investment research firm MSCI offers an opportunity to test this hypothesis. MSCI has built a world equity index of low-carbon companies. For each sector and each country, this portfolio selects assets that are best in class in terms of carbon intensity. Suppose that on September 1, 2015, I purchased such a portfolio for $1 million. And suppose also that I went short for $1 million on the standard MSCI world equity index, so that I had nothing to disburse to create this portfolio. I did that three months before the 2015 United Nations Climate Change Conference (COP 21), which took place in Paris from November 30 to December 12, 2015, and for which people had high expectations of its generating a coherent international carbon policy to efficiently fight climate change. Figure 2.1 shows the evolution of the net value of this portfolio. During COP 21, the portfolio generated a small capital gain. But although most politicians and commentators proclaimed COP 21 successful, financial markets have not been impressed at all. In fact, low-carbon assets underperformed

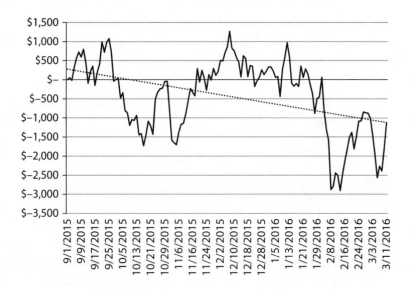

Figure 2.1 The net value of a portfolio betting on low-carbon companies.

the index afterward, and things have not gotten better since. The truth is that investors do not believe in the emergence of an efficient international policy to limit carbon emissions in the foreseeable future. And if some divestment did occur during the period, it did not depress the price of carbon-intensive companies. Either the divestment has been too marginal to be felt by markets or other less responsible investors took their place. The bottom line is that the divestment movement did not generate the anticipated effect of raising the cost of capital of irresponsible companies to incentivize them to internalize the cost of climate change. In short, it had no real effect. This is depressing.

There are, however, some reasons to believe that "one can do well by doing good" when investing one's own savings responsibly. For example, a better management of human resources that smoothes wages and hoards labor within a firm across the business cycle is certainly a good thing for workers, but also for the employer. Indeed, by offering such an implicit insurance to its employees, the firm will become more attractive to the most talented potential workers on the market, thereby improving profitability. Or, raising wages may better motivate current employees to improve productivity, as explained in the literature on "efficient wages" (Shapiro and Stiglitz 1984).

SUMMARY

Because most individual and collective actions entail costs and benefits that are different in nature, their evaluation requires the use of a common unit to compare and aggregate them. The monetary value of nonmonetary impacts is typically used for this purpose. It is measured by an individual's marginal willingness to pay for accepting or eliminating these impacts. If they are traded in efficient markets, their private value equals the observed price. The existence of public goods and various externalities implies that some determinants of individual well-being cannot be directly observed on markets. The hedonic valuation technique can sometimes allow us to observed private valuation indirectly.

Cost–benefit analysis is a method used to determine whether an action results in more benefits than costs. In most cases, an action that passes the cost–benefit analysis test generates winners and losers. If the winners do not compensate the losers, the action will not be mutually agreed upon and may generate a NIMBY effect. Moreover, in its traditional version, cost–benefit analysis simply compares the costs and the benefits of an action by using the earlier discussed values of nonmonetary impacts. However, these private values are potentially highly impacted by inequalities. More specifically, the classic cost–benefit analysis is a test of whether an action increases a weighted utilitarian welfare function, in which the weight ascribed to wealthier people is larger than that ascribed to those less wealthy. This is unfair. Alternatively, if one uses an egalitarian (unweighted) welfare function, the cost–benefit analysis test includes a concern for the reduction of inequalities.

3

DO WE DO ENOUGH FOR THE FUTURE?

One of the most crucial prices in our decentralized economies is the real interest rate. In essence, it tells us what the value is today of a representative bundle of goods and services to be delivered in the future. In its short-term version, it's mostly determined and controlled by central banks, as it influences most decisions to invest and to save. If the interest rate is 4 percent per year, the present value of a monetary benefit of $1 million that will materialize in two hundred years is $335. Thus, a simple cost–benefit analysis would induce us to reject a project that would yield a benefit of $1 million in two hundred years if it were to cost us more than $335 today. The discounting operation behind the computation of present values exponentially compresses the weight of future impacts in the evaluation of our present actions. This raises various challenges. Michael Greenstone, chief economist for President Obama's Council of Economic Advisors, stated in Greenstone, Kopits, and Wolverton (2013) that "the choice of a discount rate over especially long periods of time raises highly contested and exceedingly difficult questions of science, economics, philosophy, and law." In this chapter, I explore the normative determinants of the rate at which one should discount the future.

Although this price is the outcome of supply and demand for capital, it has a deeply normative flavor since it determines what share of current production is used for immediate consumption and what is left for the future in the form of savings and investments. In other words, it determines what we do today for the future. So the question this chapter will explore is whether this equilibrium interest rate is at a socially desirable level. Is it too low, thereby forcing current generations to sacrifice their own well-being for the benefit of future generations by investing a large fraction of current production into productive assets? Or is it too high, generating short-termism in financial markets and among their participants?

The importance of this issue can be illustrated in the context of climate change. Nordhaus (2008) uses a discount rate of 5 percent to estimate the present value of the flow of future damages (financial and extra-financial) induced by the emission of one ton of carbon dioxide today, assuming the absence of public intervention to reduce these emissions in the future. Using a sophisticated assessment model that combines economics and climate sciences, he gets a present value of these future climate damages of around $8. This means that an action to reduce carbon dioxide emissions should be undertaken only if it costs less than $8 per ton of emissions. Under these conditions, most environmental projects (such as carbon sequestration, wind power, photovoltaics, and biofuels, for example) have a negative net present value; that is, they destroy value since the immediate sacrifices required for their implementation exceed the present value of future eliminated damages. Nordhaus concludes that the best response to the climate challenge is not to invest heavily using current technologies, but rather to invest in the R&D of more efficient technologies before attempting to reduce emissions. Stern (2007) instead uses the much lower discount rate of 1.4 percent, and as a consequence, arrives at a much larger present value of future damages of around $85. With the avoided ton of carbon dioxide set at such a value, many green technologies become socially desirable. This estimation supports the immediate imposition of a tax on carbon emissions at $85 per ton to induce all economic agents on the planet to internalize this social cost of carbon. This public intervention would align private interests with the common good. In particular, it would make many actions to reduce emissions privately profitable.

THE OPPORTUNITY COST OF CAPITAL

Most investments to reduce carbon dioxide emissions require capital, and capital is scarce and costly. Thus, the speed at which our economies will undergo an energy transition depends upon the cost of capital. The interest rate is the rate of return that an investor can obtain by investing in the safest fixed-income assets, typically sovereign bonds. It sets the minimum rate of return at which investors are willing to invest in risk-free projects in the economy. If the interest rate is 4 percent, entrepreneurs will be able to finance safe projects in frictionless markets through loans at 4 percent. Hence, their cost of capital will also be 4 percent, incentivizing them to invest in projects with an internal rate of return of at least 4 percent. Thus, the interest rate is also the rate of return of the marginal safe capital invested in the economy. This is also the opportunity cost of safe capital in the economy, in the sense that any divestment of safe capital will cost the interest rate. Therefore, any new safe project financed by divesting safe capital from other sectors of the economy is socially desirable only if its internal rate of return is at least equal to the interest rate. In other words, a safe project is socially desirable only if its net present value is positive, with a discount rate equaling the interest rate.

For example, suppose that a short-lived green investment brings a benefit of $102 next year for $100 invested today and that the interest rate on markets is 4 percent. This green investment is not desirable, either privately or socially. First, if one borrows $100 on the market to finance the project, one will have to pay back $104 next year, thereby generating a loss of $2. Thus, the project is certainly not privately profitable. At the collective level, the interest rate is also the rate of return of capital in the economy, so this $100 loan is capital that cannot be invested elsewhere in the economy. The green investment generates $102 next year, but other project would have generated $104 with the same initial investment. Finally, we see that the net present value of this project equals $-100 + (102 \div 1.04) = -\$1.92$, which is negative.

The net present value of an investment measures its creation of value. It equals the immediate increase in consumption that has the same effect on intertemporal welfare as the flow of net benefits generated by the investment. Thus, investing in a safe project with a negative net present value—that is, with an internal rate of return less than the interest rate—destroys value. Put another way, more future benefits could have been created with the same sacrifice today if only one would have invested in the safe productive capital of the economy rather than in this project.

For consumers, the interest rate is the rate at which they can lend or borrow to transfer consumption over time—consuming less today (saving) and more in the future, or consuming more today (borrowing) and less in the future. But people have many other ways to transfer consumption over time. For example, they can spend more time on their education, which implies lower incomes today but hopefully larger incomes in the future. Or, they can self-finance an investment in photovoltaic panels for their roof in order to reduce their electricity bill in the future. This raises the question of a household's willingness to transfer consumption through time. It has been observed that people require more than $100 of increased consumption next year to compensate for a reduction of consumption by $100 this year. Suppose, for example, that a person needs $102 next year to accept this intertemporal transfer. In economics jargon, we would say that, in this case, the intertemporal rate of substitution is 1.02. This person would therefore be glad to save more since the current interest rate of 4 percent offers them $104. They will save more as long as the intertemporal rate of substitution is less than the interest rate. Thus, at capital market equilibrium, the interest rate will

Table 3.1 Real Return on Government Bills (annualized, in percent)

	2000–2014	1965–2014	1900–2014
China	0.7		
France	0.5	0.7	–2.8
Germany	0.5	1.7	–2.4
Japan	0.1	0.3	–1.9
United Kingdom	0.1	1.4	0.9
United States	–0.4	0.9	0.9
World	–0.4	0.9	0.9

Source: Dimson, Marsh, and Staunton 2015.

reveal both the rate of return of risk-free capital in the economy and people's rate of substitution between current and future consumption.

Table 3.1 shows what the real interest rate on government bills has been for the last 15, 50, and 115 years prior to the end of 2014 for twenty-three different countries and in the world (for a U.S. investor). Bills are short-term debt contracts with a maturity of less than a year. Over the last century, the real short-term interest rate has been around 1 percent, with large cross-country variations and has been negative in most countries that experienced a World War on their soil. But if we limit the analysis to the last 15 years, the average real interest rate has been on average negative, partly because of the "global saving glut" generated by the high saving rates observed in emerging economies.

Returns are typically larger when considering safe assets with longer maturities, as can be seen in Table 3.2. According to Dimson, Marsh, and Staunton (2015), twenty-year

Table 3.2 Real Return on Twenty-Year Government Bonds (annualized, in percent)

	2000–2014	1965–2014	1900–2014
China	3.0		
France	6.6	5.9	0.2
Germany	7.5	4.9	–1.4
Japan	3.9	4.4	–0.9
United Kingdom	3.6	3.2	1.6
United States	6.0	3.4	2.0
World	5.5	4.3	1.9

Source: Dimson, Marsh, and Staunton 2015.

Treasury bonds in the United States had an annualized rate of return of 2 percent over the period from 1900 to 2014. The long-term interest rate was high in the period from 1990 to 2007. But King and Low (2014) estimated that the weighted mean of the ten-year interest rate in the world has been almost 0 percent since 2012.

Globally, these observations suggest a relative resistance to the transfer of consumption through time. People have saved quite a bit in spite of the very low rate of return of saving during the last century. These observations also suggest that markets provide strong incentives to invest for the future, at least in the safest projects. For example, in the United States on average during the period from 1900 to 2014, it was socially desirable to invest in all ten-year risk-free projects whose annualized returns were greater than 2 percent, which is a relatively low requirement.

CREDIT MARKETS FAILURES

Credit markets allow people with profitable investment opportunities to trade with people who face excess saving capabilities. The interest rate can be interpreted as the price of time that balances the demand and supply of capital in the economy. In a frictionless economy, the interest rate reveals both the opportunity cost of capital and an individual's willingness to delay consumption. This double identification characterizes an efficient intertemporal allocation of resources, in the sense that it leads to maximum intertemporal welfare. This theoretical result is parallel to the result discussed in chapter 2 that competition on the apples market leads to an efficient allocation of apples in the economy, and that the price of apples provides the right signal for consumers and producers of apples to determine their choice in line with the common good. Does this interest rate decentralize an efficient dynamic allocation of consumption?

Credit markets face multiple sources of friction arising from the difficulty lenders face in evaluating the creditworthiness of potential borrowers. These frictions lead to an inefficient allocation of resources and to an equilibrium interest rate that doesn't give agents the right price signals; that is, those that align their private interests with the common good when determining their saving and investment decisions. This is due in particular to the fact that financial markets are affected by various agency problems. Investment financing of businesses and individuals is made difficult by the fact that lenders generally have insufficient information on borrowers' repayment capacity (Stiglitz and Weiss 1981).

Investment financing is also affected by moral hazard when lenders cannot control borrowers' exposure to risk. For example, a highly leveraged bank with a low solvency ratio may be tempted to "bet for resurrection" by taking excessive risk, given the fact that most of the downside risk will be borne by the creditors of the bank in case of failure (Jensen and Meckling 1976). The adverse selection and moral hazard problems that this generates in the financial markets are very important, as suggested by the repetition of crises (e.g., the subprime bubble, the Internet bubble, the sovereign debt crisis) that these markets face. In addition to the significant inefficiencies in the allocation of capital in the economy, these problems cause distortions in market prices.

These inefficiencies are particularly prevalent in developing countries. Poor farmers don't have much collateral to guarantee loans, and banks often face high costs to recover small loans in the countryside. The consequences are catastrophic, both for the farmers and for the economy as a whole. Loans cannot be used in bad times to smooth the shock of a bad harvest that puts the population on the verge of starvation. Because such adverse events are systematic in the sense that they often hit all farmers at the same time, local risk-sharing and solidarity do not work well to manage crop risks. During these critical periods, individuals are willing to borrow at almost any interest rate, and credit sharks are often there to offer usury loans. Moreover, in normal times, farmers can take actions to improve their future that require some sacrifices in the short run. Purchasing a cow, a plow, or some fertilizer can generate a large return by improving agricultural productivity. But these investments often remain unexploited because of the credit constraints these farmers face, constraints that drastically limit their hopes for a better life. These constraints also limit the growth of the economy. Because of these important frictions, credit markets allocate capital very inefficiently. Investments are made in poor projects, leaving some other potentially very profitable investment projects unexploited. The microcredit system initiated by the Grameen Bank, since copied around the world, is a promising avenue to make the world better. New financial technologies ("fintech") are also expected to bring banks closer to the people who need credit the most.

INTERGENERATIONAL INEFFICIENCY

Another source of inefficiency in credit market appears in an intergenerational context. As pointed out by Diamond (1977), future generations obviously cannot trade with present generations. Therefore, the interests of future generations cannot be expressed in the markets. If capital accumulation occurs, it is because young people expect themselves to accumulate assets they can later sell to fund their retirement, and also, perhaps, because they feel some altruism toward their descendants and want to transfer capital to them. Take the extreme case, in which only one selfish generation lives in each period. The competitive equilibrium would maximize a utilitarian welfare function in which all generations except the current one receive a zero weight. There would hardly be any saving, investment, or capital accumulation in such an economy. There would also be hardly any risk-sharing or

intertemporal consumption smoothing. In reality, generations are not purely selfish, and the intergenerational altruism expressed by transfers within families (e.g., investment
in education, monetary gifts to children, voluntary bequests,
elder care for parents) alleviate some of the problems of self-
ishness, together with the fact that successive generations
overlap. But intergenerational altruism is probably insufficient for the interest rate to reflect something other than the
sole interest of present generations because this altruism is
mostly limited to the family, and only to the next one or two
subsequent generations.

In the absence of yet-to-be-born generations in financial
markets, the competitive equilibrium maximizes an intergenerational welfare function in which the interests of
future generations are underrepresented. This is unfair, as
is the fact that wealthy people are over-represented in the
welfare function that supports the cost–benefit analysis
method of evaluation examined in chapter 2. Just as there
is a difference between the equilibrium outcome and the
fair, efficient one, there is a difference between the market
interest rate and the fair, efficient discount rate. Under the
veil of ignorance about the generation in which they will be
born, an impartial and rational person would evaluate the
intergenerational distribution of consumption by using an
unweighted sum of generational utilities. As a consequence,
the equilibrium interest rate emerging from overlapping-
generation models of economic growth theory is inefficient,
as is the observed interest rate in markets. Accordingly,
the equilibrium interest rate will be larger than is socially
desirable because people will ignore the benefits of their

investments accruing to future generations. People will not invest enough for the future.

Finally, interest rates have a term structure that is usually not flat: In normal time, the short-term interest rate is lower than the long-term one. For example, Tables 3.1 and 3.2 tell us that over the period from 2000 to 2014 in the United States, investors received a real annualized interest rate of only −0.4 percent if they invested in sovereign debt with a term of less than one year, but they would have obtained a real annualized interest rate of 6.0 percent if they had invested in twenty-year sovereign debt instruments. Thus, the term structure in the United States was strongly upward-shaped during that period. But the term structure can some-time be inverted, in particular before and at the beginning of an economic downturn. For example, in December 1928, the short-term and long-term nominal interest rates were 3.5 percent and 0 percent, respectively. We must therefore recognize that the arbitrage argument presented earlier in this chapter should induce us to use different discount rates for safe cash flows with different maturities. The problem is that we usually don't have truly safe assets traded on markets for maturities exceeding two or three decades. The creation of inflation-protected Treasury bonds is certainly useful in complete financial markets, but the liquidity of this asset class, which has the longest maturities, is usually too limited for the observation of a real interest rate. Creating liquid indexed sovereign bonds with maturities of one hundred or two hundred years would be useful to improve cost–benefit analyses for any public policies or long-term investments, in particular those linked to infrastructure, energy transition, climate change, nonrenewable resources, and sustainable development.

My colleague Jacques Delpla and I are trying to convince central banks and national treasury institutions to offer long-dated debt contracts. From a private point of view, this may be optimal to lock in low interest rates to finance long-term investment projects, to postpone reinvestment risk, or to reduce the cost of the public debt for a long period of time. Currently, the average debt maturity of the U.S. sovereign debt is around five years. U.S. Secretary of the Treasury Steven Mnuchin declared in November 2016 that he would like the Treasury to change that by offering fifty- and one-hundred-year securities. In the fall of 2016, Belgium offered a bond that will mature in 2116, at a rate of 2.3 percent. This is an important price signal, for example, for pension funds or companies of the nuclear industry, which have to value the long-term liabilities on their balance sheets. More generally, the observation that people are willing to have this Belgian bond in their portfolio provides important information for entrepreneurs who have very safe Belgian projects maturing in 2116: Invest in them if and only if their annual nominal return exceeds 2.3 percent!

IN A GROWING ECONOMY, INVESTING INCREASES INTERGENERATIONAL INEQUALITY

From the point of view of our impartial yet-to-be-born person, an obvious argument appears for valuing future benefits less than current benefits. Suppose we anticipate sustained positive growth. Investing in this context amounts to transferring consumption from the penurious current generation to the future generation. This transfers consumption from the poor to the wealthy; that is, it is an action that increases intergenerational inequality. If such a transfer generates an additional apple in the future for each apple sacrificed today, the investment would reduce intergenerational welfare, simply because the marginal utility of apples in the future is smaller than the marginal utility of apples today. Investing for the future is socially desirable only if the social cost of this reverse redistribution is more than offset by a sufficiently high return on investment. In other words, in a growing economy, the discount rate can be interpreted as the minimum internal rate of return of an investment that offsets the negative impact of the investment on intergenerational inequality.

With a real growth rate of consumption of 2 percent per year, we now consume fifty times more goods and services than during the Napoleonic era. If we anticipate maintaining this growth rate, the issue of climate change amounts to worrying about the welfare of people who, in two hundred years, will receive a per capita GDP that is fifty times higher than ours. From this perspective, fighting climate change is like asking Bangladeshis to donate a share of their income today to enrich the lives of people in the United States. This should be done only if the return of such actions is really large. This may well be the case for climate change. Suppose indeed that in two hundred years, people will consume fifty times more goods and services (corrected for quality) than we do. Suppose also that the elasticity of the marginal utility of income is $\gamma = 2$, as discussed in chapter 2. This means that the future marginal utility will be 2,500 times larger in two hundred years than it is today. In other words, one should accept a sacrifice of one apple today only if it generates a benefit of at least 2,500 apples in two hundred years. This safe project has a real return of at least 4 percent per year.

THE RAMSEY RULE

How can we estimate the efficient discount rate associated with this argument? Let's estimate the minimum future benefit per dollar invested today that compensates for the increased intergenerational inequality that it generates. Two ingredients are key: inequality aversion and consumption growth. Suppose that the economy grows at g percent per year and that the elasticity of marginal utility is γ. This implies that marginal utility will grow at γg percent per year. As a consequence, this must be the minimum rate of return of a safe project to increase the unweighted sum of temporal utilities. This is usually referred to as the Ramsey rule (Ramsey 1928).

Thus, if one believes that economic growth will continue to be around 2 percent per year forever, and if one takes the ethical posture of an inequality aversion of 2, we must conclude that the discount rate that is compatible with the preferences of an impartial and rational person under the veil of ignorance is 4 percent per year in real terms. In this context, an investment that would cost one apple now and generate two thousand apples in two hundred years would have a net present value of $-1 + (2{,}000 \div (1.04)^{200}) = -0.22$. It would not be a good idea to implement this investment because it would reduce social welfare. But of course, this result relies on the assumption that the beneficiaries of the investment will be fifty times wealthier than the payers.

UNCERTAINTY AND PRUDENCE

Larry Summers (2014) and Robert Gordon (2015, 2016), among others, have claimed that the most recent economic revolution arising from new information technologies did not involve much actual economic growth. They have claimed the world is instead facing the risk of a century of stagnation; that is, a "secular stagnation." The low growth rate experienced in the West since the 2008 financial crisis is here to stay, following Summers' and Gordon's dismal predictions. Following Gordon (2015), productivity growth has clearly slowed in the United States. Part of this slowdown reflects the productivity growth decline to diminishing returns in the digital revolution that had its peak effect in the late 1990s, but which has resulted in little change in business hardware, software, or best practices since. To illustrate the loss in the growth component of innovation, consider a thought experiment in which you have to decide whether to give up sanitation (an innovation from the latter half of the nineteenth century) or the Internet in your home. When I ask my students this question, all except a few extreme geeks say they would prefer to give up the Internet. This illustrates that the Internet has had a smaller impact on our welfare—and thus on economic growth—than sanitation.

This is in line with the observed reduction in the real-world interest rate documented by King and Low (2014), mentioned earlier. With the dearth of attractive investment opportunities, the long-term interest rate must go down for the reduced demand for capital to meet households' supply of savings. At the same time, many households realize that they must save more because the anticipated growth of their income may not materialize owing to the prolonged crisis. These combined forces tend to push interest rates down permanently, which could ignite a vicious circle in which people save more because of the low return of their pension plans. The increase in saving may push interest rates down further, yielding a new wave of increased saving. In the absence of any new wave of technological revolution, secular growth prospects are thus bleak. According to this "diminishing expectations" theory, it would be socially desirable to use a lower discount rate to evaluate safe long-term projects. This is precisely what the Ramsey rule tells us to do.

However, the worst is never certain. Throughout history, societies have faced shocks, sometimes very violent and long-lasting, that have profoundly affected their history. China, which was the most developed region in the world in the fifteenth century, found itself among the poorest in the last two centuries until its current extraordinary comeback. The West has known the prosperity and collapse of the Roman Empire, followed by what was essentially a long, stagnant period until before the Industrial Revolution. According to Clark (2007), the daily wage in Babylon in the middle of the second millennium b.c. was fifteen pounds of wheat. During the Golden Age of ancient Greece under Pericles, it was twenty-six pounds of wheat. In England around 1780, it was just thirteen pounds of wheat. This illustrates that economic growth was essentially nonexistent for four millennia. And many historians believe the agricultural revolution of the Neolithic Era reduced rather than increased standards of living compared with those experienced by hunters and gatherers. One possible explanation for this is that the Neolithic revolution was made possible only through the creation of the notion of private ownership (e.g., in terms of things like land and seeds). This was possible only in association with a strong centralization of power to protect ownership rights, implying high administrative and military costs. Moreover, because of Malthus's law, the productivity gains of the agricultural revolution were translated into population growth rather than into an increase in individual welfare.

The shock of the Industrial Revolution and an improvement in the control of human fertility transformed an almost zero-growth trend over several millennia to a growth trend of 2 percent per year in the Western world. Who can say whether this is a temporary aberration of history or a new and lasting reality? Those who warn of an inevitable decline evoke the disappearance of nonrenewable resources (especially fossil fuels), the end of scientific discoveries, major health crises, and so on. Optimists support the idea of sustained development through the conquest of space or through scientific and technological innovations, particularly in the areas of green energy, digital technology, biotechnology, and genetics.

The truth is that the future is inherently uncertain, and this truth is central to how we should judge our responsibilities toward future generations. It is nonsense to evaluate long-dated investment projects on the hypothesis of a stable 2 percent growth rate in our economy forever. The deep uncertainty attached to the distant future cannot be ignored. Any policy decision regarding the sustainability of development must take into account the considerable uncertainty in our collective future.

How should this uncertainty affect our responsibilities toward the future? In order to determine a principle of collective decision-making, we need to re-examine the problem the impartial, rational decision-maker faces under the veil of ignorance.

How should uncertainty about the future affect how we evaluate actions aimed at improving things in the future? Again, let's think about this problem through introspection. Suppose that *your* future income will become more uncertain, with both upside and downside risks. Would you react to this uncomfortable news in terms of your efforts to make your future better? One example of these efforts is savings. We know that households increase their "precautionary" savings when they're uncertain about future income, accumulating more wealth to better face times of uncertainty. This hypothesis, first proposed by John Maynard Keynes, has since been systematically evaluated through econometric studies (see, for example, Guiso, Jappelli, and Terlizzese 1996). Since the work of Leland (1968) and Drèze and Modigliani (1972), we have known that this behavioral assumption of prudence holds if, and only if, marginal utility is a convex function of consumption. Indeed, if marginal utility is convex, introducing a zero-mean risk on future consumption increases expected marginal utility. The downside risk has a larger positive impact on marginal utility than the upside one. From this arises the value of investing today to increase future consumption.

To illustrate, if inequality aversion equals 2, we know that, in order to give $1 to the poor, one should be willing to give up as much as $4 from another person whose revenue is twice the revenue of the poor. Alternatively, assume that the revenue of the wealthy is uncertain. It is either the same or three times greater than that of the poor. Although nothing has changed in expectation, the expected marginal utility of the wealthy is now only 5/9 of the marginal utility of the poor. In other words, in this uncertain context, one should not be willing to sacrifice more than $1.80 from the wealthy to give $1 to the poor. The uncertainty about how much wealthier the wealthy will be reduces the power of the inequality aversion argument. This precautionary argument is increasing in the degree of convexity of marginal utility, which is referred to as the degree of "prudence." When the elasticity of marginal utility is a constant γ, the degree of prudence is also a constant and is equal to $\gamma+1$.

Eeckhoudt and Schlesinger (2006) propose a simple test to determine if our preferences follow this prudent hypothesis. Prudent people, people whose marginal utility is convex, exhibit a preference for the disaggregation of "harms." Consider, for example, two harms: a sure loss of $100 and the addition of a zero-mean lottery (e.g., a lottery with an equal probability of winning or losing $100). Consider lottery L_1, in which you will receive one of these two "harms" for sure, the only uncertainty being which one. The alternative is

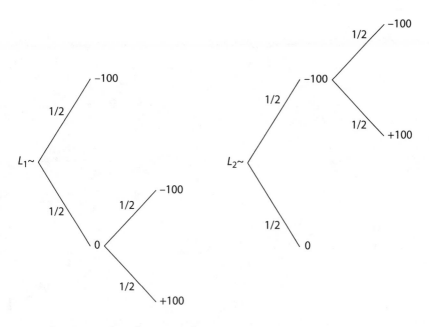

Figure 3.1 A choice between two lotteries.

lottery L_2, in which you have a fifty-fifty chance of receiving both harms simultaneously or receiving neither, as shown in figure 3.1. Compounding probabilities, these two lotteries can be represented as shown in figure 3.2. Notice that the two lotteries have the same expected payoff and the same variance. Notice also that lottery L_1 is positively skewed, whereas lottery L_2 is negatively skewed.

It is intuitive that one would prefer lottery L_1. Eeckhoudt and Schlesinger (2006) have shown that this preference characterizes prudent people. I consider this to be a pervasive argument in favor of prudence and of the convexity of the marginal utility of consumption. It is noteworthy that

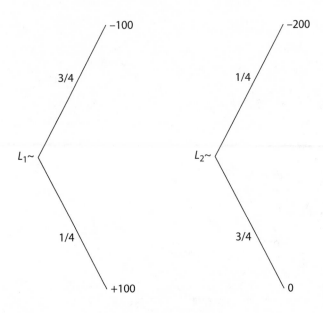

Figure 3.2 A simpler representation of the two lotteries.

prudence links the notion of precautionary savings with the preference for positively skewed lotteries. An extreme version of such lotteries is the EuroMillions, in which gamblers are almost sure to lose their bet, but there is a very small probability of becoming a millionaire. This kind of lottery is generally more attractive than those in which the best outcome is a more likely but smaller payoff.

To sum up, when economic growth is uncertain but positive in expectation, two competing mechanisms determine the socially desirable discount rate. Because we expect future generations to be wealthier, it is socially desirable to require the discount rate to be high enough to compensate for the increased intergenerational inequality that investing generates. This is an argument for investing less and for recommending a positive discount rate. But the uncertainty about the intensity and direction of the intergenerational inequality should induce prudent communities to invest more in riskless projects. This precautionary argument tends to reduce the socially desirable discount rate. In theory, this argument may even dominate the inequality aversion argument to yield a negative discount rate. This could be the case if the probability that future generations end up worse off compared with our own generation is high enough. In such a case, one should be willing to invest in safe projects with a negative return. Markets and the European Central Bank have induced people to do so over the last few years when the real interest rate in the Eurozone was negative. This also occurred in several European countries over the last century when real interest rates were deep into negative territory.

Technically, a sure investment that generates a benefit b in t years per dollar invested today increases intergenerational welfare if, and only if, the utility cost $U'(c_0)$ today is smaller than the utility benefit at date t, which is measured by $bEU'(c_t)$. This condition is equivalent to requiring that net present value, measured by $-1+b\exp(-rt)$, be positive, where $\exp(-rt) = EU'(c_t)/U'(c_0)$ is the discount factor and r is the discount rate.

THE BROWNIAN WORLD

Prudence is an attractive feature of our collective preferences. In an uncertain world, it should induce us to do more for the future. As noted earlier, using a discount rate of 4 percent to evaluate safe projects (as suggested by the Ramsey rule) implies that only those impacts that will materialize within two or three decades are relevant to determining net present value. By how much could this short-termism be tempered by prudence?

In finance and macroeconomics, the traditional way to model the uncertainty surrounding our collective destiny is to assume that consumption per capita follows a geometric Brownian process. This means that, at every instant, the instantaneous growth rate of consumption is normally distributed with mean μ and is independent of what happened in the past. Shocks to the growth rate are thus very short-lived. The annualized volatility σ of this growth rate is a simple measure of the uncertainty affecting the future. It implies that the consumption per capita at any future time t, denoted c_t, is log-normally distributed with mean μt and variance $\sigma^2 t$.

In the technical appendix, I show that the volatility of the growth rate reduces the risk-free discount rate by $0.5\gamma^2\sigma^2$, which is a precautionary premium. This risk premium is a constant independent of the maturity of the benefit. Let's calibrate this using U.S. data. Over the last two centuries, the trend of consumption growth has been 2 percent per year. With an inequality aversion of $\gamma = 2$, the Ramsey rule suggests using a discount rate of 4 percent. The annualized volatility of this growth rate of consumption has been around 3 percent. Extrapolating this Gaussian uncertainty to the future implies a reduction of the discount rate by $0.5 \times 2^2 \times (3\%)^2$, which is approximately 0.2 percent. This implies, in turn, a reduction of the discount rate from 4 percent to 3.8 percent. The effect of uncertainty is surprisingly low within this framework. This is clearly very disappointing if we are hoping that uncertainty will make us more long-term oriented, and I consider this to be a "long-termism puzzle." The intergenerational aversion argument to fix the discount rate seems too much more powerful—by at least one degree of magnitude—than the precautionary argument.

Moreover, observe that, in this Gaussian world, the socially desirable discount rate is independent of the time horizon at which the sure benefit under evaluation materializes. In other words, if it is socially desirable to discount short-term safe benefits at 3.8 percent per year, it is also optimal to discount sure benefits occurring in two centuries at the same rate. The term structure of the socially desirable discount rate is totally flat.

The comparison of this recommended discount rate of 3.8 percent with the observed average interest rate of between 1 percent and 2 percent in the United States since 1900 leads to the so-called risk-free rate puzzle (Weil 1989). In a frictionless economy, the interest rate is the minimum rate of return at which investors and entrepreneurs are willing to invest in risk-free assets and projects. This means that, during the last century, previous generations invested a much more in safe projects than they should have to maximize intergenerational welfare. As the story goes, given how wealthy we are today compared with our grandparents, these past generations sacrificed far too much of their own revenue to finance long-term infrastructure, R&D, and education. The extraordinary accumulation of capital they offered us is inefficient from the point of view of intergenerational welfare. So, if one believes that we live in a Gaussian world, past generations did too much for us. Collectively, it would have been more desirable for previous generations to save less and consume more of the wealth they produced. From this point of view, markets for fixed-income assets have been too long-termist—not short-termist—in the United States. If we were to duplicate this analysis for other Western countries, we would obtain roughly the same result.

AN INTERNATIONAL PERSPECTIVE

Some poor countries have experienced a dismal economic dynamic over the last few decades. For example, over the period from 1961 to 2015, the annual growth rate of GDP per capita in the Democratic Republic of the Congo has been *minus* 1.3 percent per year on average, with a volatility of around 5 percent. The Ramsey rule extended to risk yields a discount rate of *minus* 3 percent. Similar negative discount rates would also prevail in Haiti, Nicaragua, Tajikistan, Niger, and Togo, for example. This strange result comes from the basic assumption we have made here, which is that each country is endowed with its own "eternal" growth dynamic characterized by constant trend and volatility. If this were true, the growth data from the Democratic Republic of the Congo would suggest that these countries will soon decline back to the Stone Age.

In such cases, the argument for inequality aversion goes in the opposite direction. Because current generations are wealthier, they should invest even in projects with negative returns because investing for the future has the additional benefit of reducing intergenerational inequalities. The precautionary effect reinforces this recommendation. But this result is implicitly a consequence of the assumption that each country faces its own Brownian motion, with no interaction with other countries. International trade, product imitation, and various positive externalities (e.g., medication, knowledge) coming from the growth of other countries should influence the destiny of the poorest regions of the world, which should eventually catch up in terms of standard of living.

This idea can be illustrated by China, which had both a mean growth rate and a volatility of growth of 7 percent over the same period, from 1961 to 2015. Using the same method, the socially desirable discount rate in China should be around 13 percent. Given the enormous intergenerational inequalities that this growth rate suggests, saving and investing for the future make no sense under the veil of ignorance, because future generations will be so much wealthier. But the fact is that Chinese households save a lot. According to data from the Organisation for Economic Co-operation and Development (OECD), China both saved and reinvested 49 percent of its GDP in 2015 versus the United States with a savings rate of 19 percent.

One possible explanation for the situation in China is that the country's beliefs about the its economic growth integrate information not contained in the recent growth data. For example, some people may believe that the Chinese economy will soon crash, necessitating precautionary saving.

This is a reasonable notion, given the variability the Chinese economy has seen over the centuries. China went from being one of the most developed regions of the world in the sixteenth century to being one of the poorest by the middle of the twentieth century, only to start an unprecedented comeback in recent years. Because extreme events like this are very rare in a Gaussian world, such variability suggests we need to enrich the way we described the long-run uncertainty described earlier before making policy recommendations. This is our objective for the remainder of this chapter. The Brownian hypothesis is far too crude to reasonably describe our collective beliefs for the destiny of human beings on this planet. No tree grows to the sky.

In the long run, it is likely that the world's economies will converge toward a more uniform level of development, thanks to trade, technological transfers, and learning from the inefficiencies of failed states. If we believe in long-term convergence, we should recognize that poorer countries have better growth prospects, which implies that discount rates should be relatively higher in these countries. In a frictionless economy, all agents should use the same rate to discount riskless benefits occurring at any specific future date, but frictions on international capital markets violate this law, because risk-free capital cannot be transferred to regions where it creates more value. The heterogeneity of the socially desirable discount rate across countries explains why it is so difficult to achieve international consensus on the social cost of carbon. In fast-growing countries in the South, the higher long-term discount rate implies more short-termism—and a lower social cost of carbon—than in the North. In this sense, imposing the fight against climate change as a top international priority over other problems involving more immediate benefits, such as improving workplace safety in Bangladesh, improving sanitation in Zimbabwe, or fighting human immunodeficiency virus (HIV) and malaria in Sub-Saharan Africa, for example, could appear to be a new form of imperialism. Different attitudes toward the future, and the associated differences in country-specific discount rates, should be recognized by international institutions as a byproduct of the world inequality of growth prospects and of the fragmentation of financial markets. These differences should be treated with respect in international relations.

BUSINESS CYCLES: NEVER LOSE THE LONG-TERM PERSPECTIVE

The simplest way to generalize the unrealistic Brownian hypothesis is to allow the trend μ of growth to vary over time, as in Bansal and Yaron (2004). Our economies are subject to cycles in which recessions are followed by booms that can last several years. The Great Depression suppressed growth for more than a decade on both side of the Atlantic, and Europe is still suffering from very weak growth ten years after the beginning of the financial crisis of 2008. In other words, the shock to the consumption growth rate exhibits some persistence. This is usually modeled by allowing the growth trend to follow another Brownian motion with a reversion to the mean. The immediate consequence of mean reversion is that growth expectations become cyclical. It is thus desirable that the short-term discount rate also be cyclical. In periods of declining expectations, the inequality argument is weakened. In the extreme case in which a recession is expected, the short-term discount rate should be negative because the inequality argument is reversed in such cases and goes hand in hand with the precautionary argument. On the other hand, if a boom is expected, the inequality argument is magnified, and the short-term discount rate should be increased. Typically, market interest rates follow the same procyclical pattern.

But this enrichment of the stochastic structure of the consumption dynamic has almost no effect on the rate at which long-term impacts should be discounted. The reason for this is quite simple. Because the trend always reverses to its historical mean, the expected annualized growth rate tends to this historical mean by the law of large numbers. So, contrary to its short-run impact, the intensity of the inequality argument is not affected by the cyclicality of the growth trend. The persistence of shocks introduces some positive correlation in annual growth rate, which increases the variance of distant consumption and thus the intensity of the precautionary argument. But any realistic calibration of this mean reversion in the Western world indicates that this effect is only marginal. Mean reversion cannot solve the long-termism puzzle.

A clear message emerges from this analysis. Because the discount rate for far distant impacts is unaffected by booms and recessions, our evaluation of long-term projects is mostly independent of the current economic situation. In short, a bad economic context should not be an excuse to postpone actions with long-term benefits. Our responsibilities toward future generations cannot be ignored because of our short-term problems. But it is also true that at the beginning of an economic downturn, short-term discount rates should be low, and even negative in the worst scenarios. The increasing term structure of discount rate that emerges in this context illustrates the need to invest more in safe projects that have immediate benefits to alleviate the forthcoming downturn. But this should not mean that we stop financing actions with extra-long impacts.

WE WILL PROBABLY NOT EXPERIENCE AN INDUSTRIAL-ERA LEVEL OF ECONOMIC GROWTH FOREVER

One of the bad habits of economists, politicians, business leaders, and individuals is to extrapolate the future from the most recent past. On the timescale of humanity, the "recent" past consists of what has happened since the Industrial Revolution. This period was characterized by a large growth rate in consumption and low macroeconomic volatility. But does it make sense to extrapolate what happened during the last two centuries to determine our moral responsibilities toward all future generations of people who will inhabit Earth?

Integrating the entire history of growth forces us to reconsider this approach. The economic history of the world has one striking feature: for thousands of years, per capita consumption remained close to subsistence level, with basically no growth at all. Volatility existed, with periods of relative prosperity (e.g., the Roman Empire, the Renaissance) followed by periods of misery (e.g., the Black Death, the Thirty Years' War), but the average consumption growth over the past seven millennia has been zero. Then came the Industrial Revolution with its 2 percent average consumption growth rate. Since we have seen such an upward regime switch in the past, another quasi-permanent regime switch—either upward or downward—is plausible in the future. In particular, as suggested by the current debate on secular stagnation, nobody can be sure about the trend of growth for the next century or millennium. Random regime switches are not impossible.

In *Pricing the Planet's Future* (Gollier 2012), I explored the consequence of modeling the long-run dynamic of economic growth as a Markovian–Brownian process. This model includes two possible regimes of growth. In the good regime, economic growth is Brownian, as described earlier, with a trend of 2 percent and a volatility of 3.6 percent. In the bad regime, economic growth is also Brownian, but with a trend of 0 percent. The model also assumes that every year, there is a 1 percent probability of switching from the current regime to the other regime.

Suppose that, in spite of the low growth we have experienced since the financial crisis of 2008, we optimistically believe that we are still in the good regime. In this case, socially desirable discount rates have a decreasing term structure. For short-term costs and benefits, the risk of regime switch is too small to affect the rate at which these cash flows should be discounted. The short-term discount rate is approximately 3.8 percent. But the picture is completely different for the valuation of the distant impacts of today's actions; the socially desirable discount rate for a one-hundred-year maturity goes down to 2 percent. For cash flows occurring in two centuries or more, the discount rate drops further, to 1 percent. There are two reasons for this low asymptotic level of discount rates. First, the probability of a switch from the good regime to the bad should reduce our expectations about the growth of consumption. This weakens the inequality argument. In fact, in the very long run, the average growth rate is only 1 percent. The Ramsey rule thus suggests using $2 \times 1\% = 2\%$ to discount extra-long impacts. But the risk of regime switch at an uncertain date considerably magnifies the uncertainty surrounding far distant consumption levels. Our estimation of future expected marginal utility in this context tells us that the asymptotic discount rate should be reduced further, by one hundred basis points, to 1 percent.

DEEP UNCERTAINTY

But, in fact, we face deeper uncertainties concerning the distant future. Even in the short run, experts disagree about how fast our economy will grow. This means that there is some fundamental uncertainty about economic growth, and this uncertainty increases exponentially when considering longer time horizons. The probabilities of the different long-term economic scenarios are ambiguous. But if we are collectively unable to characterize a unique probability distribution to describe our uncertain collective destiny, how can we evaluate our actions to fulfill our duties toward future generations?

A simple way to describe ambiguous probabilities is by introducing a second-order risk into the model. Suppose the growth rate of consumption exhibits no serial correlation and is stationary. In other words, every year, the annual growth rate is randomly selected from the same unknown probability distribution. To keep the story simple, suppose there are only two possible annual growth rates, H or L, with H being greater than L. Every year, the annual growth rate is determined by drawing a ball from an urn. The ball is returned to the urn for a further independent draw the next year. We know there are two types of balls in the urn, but we don't know their proportion; that is, we don't know the probability of drawing either H or L. Following Savage (1954), one should form some beliefs about the true distribution of the balls in the urn to rationalize our decisions under this uncertainty. Jakob Bernoulli's principle of insufficient reason suggests that, in the absence of any additional information about the composition of the urn, one should assume the probability of drawing either H or L is equal to 0.5. If we believe this, a flat term structure of discount rates is socially desirable, as in the Brownian case described earlier.

Suppose, alternatively, that you believe there are two urns to draw from, with an equal probability of drawing from either one: a good urn, with a 90 percent chance of drawing an H ball, and a bad urn, with a 10 percent chance of drawing an H ball. In expectation, these beliefs are also unbiased. But in this framework, the decision-maker now faces two sources of risk: the first-order risk of drawing a ball from an urn, and the second-order risk of the uncertain composition of the urn. This second-order risk is described by the uncertain probability of H, which is either 0.9 or 0.1, with an equal probability of selecting either. Because expected utility is linear in probabilities, using a sure probability of 0.5 or this uncertain probability with the same mean would make no difference in estimating the rate at which one should discount a benefit occurring in one year. However, because the structure of the true probability of H is constant (but unknown), we have an element of persistence that radically transforms our vision of the more distant future.

Consider the probability of observing two consecutive bad draws during the first two years. If we assume the probability of L is 0.5, the probability of two bad draws is $(1/2)^2 = 25\%$. But if the probability is uncertain (as assumed earlier), then the true probability of observing a sequence of two bad draws is either $(0.9)^2$ or $(0.1)^2$. The expected probability is thus 41 percent, which is greater than 25 percent. The risks associated with two-year growth, with and without probability ambiguity, are depicted in figure 3.3. More generally, as shown by Halevy and Feltkamp (2005), the ambiguity affecting probabilities raises the expected probability of extreme events when independent draws are added up to determine the final outcome.

Things are even worse when contemplating the three-year horizons, in which the probability of observing three bad draws is 12.5 percent if the probability of a bad draw is a sure 0.5 and the expected probability is 36.5 percent if the probability of a bad draw is uncertain. The uncertainty affecting the annual growth probabilities magnifies the long-run risk.

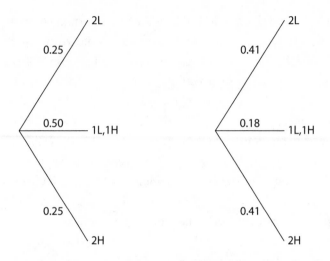

Figure 3.3 The risk associated with two-year growth when the independent annual growth rates are either H or L, with probability p and 1 − p, respectively. In the left graph, p is known to be equal to ½. In the right graph, p is unknown but has an equal probability of being either 0.1 or 0.9.

Prudent people should react by using a lower rate to discount sure benefits occurring in the more distant future.

Suppose, more specifically, that if an H ball is drawn from the urn, the growth rate of the coming year will be 4 percent, whereas there will be no growth at all during the coming year if an L ball is drawn. Suppose first that the proportion of H and L balls in the urn is known to be 50:50. With an inequality aversion index of 2, it is easy to verify that a constant discount rate of 3.9 percent should be used for all maturities.[1] But if we don't know whether the true composition of the urn is 10:90 or 90:10, the picture is quite different. Because the ambiguity affecting probabilities has no effect on the

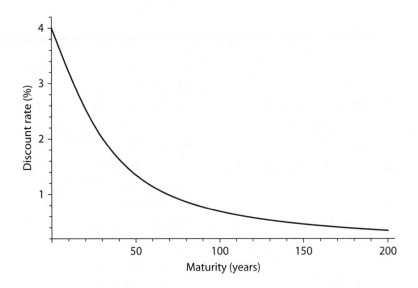

Figure 3.4 The term structure of risk-free discount rates (in percent per year) as a function of the maturity of the sure benefit to be discounted. I have assumed an inequality aversion of 2, and an independent, identically distributed annual growth rate of either 2 percent per year with probability p or 0 percent with probability 1 − p. Probability p has an equal probability of being either 0.1 or 0.9.

measure of the short-term risk but magnifies the long-term risk as shown in figure 3.3, prudence justifies distorting our preferences in favor of safe projects yielding benefits in the distant future. This is done by using lower discount rates for longer maturities. Figure 3.4 illustrates the term structure of efficient risk-free discount rates in this context. For short maturities, a discount rate of around 3.9 percent remains socially desirable, but for longer maturities, a lower discount rate converging on zero is optimal.

This rule is technically similar to a formula proposed by Weitzman (1998, 2001) in another context. It is easy to show that, whatever the structure of the uncertainty, the efficient discount rate has a decreasing term structure, and it goes down to the lowest discount rate compatible with the possible true distribution of growth for large maturities.

In Gollier (2008), I assume that economic growth follows a geometric Brownian motion, with a known volatility σ and a constant trend μ, which is uncertain. I also assume that our belief about this trend is normally distributed with mean μ_0 and standard deviation σ_0. This parameter measures the ambiguity affecting growth probabilities. In this case, the consumption per capita at any future time t, denoted c_t, is lognormally distributed with mean μt and variance $\sigma^2 t + \sigma_0^2 t^2$. The only difference—compared with the standard Brownian case with no uncertainty in the trend—is the presence of this quadratic term in the variance. It confirms that the ambiguity on probabilities has no effect for short maturities but is critically important in evaluating investments with long-lasting impacts.

In fact, this model implies a term structure of the risk-free discount rate that decreases *linearly* with maturity. For sufficiently long maturities, the discount rate is negative. It tends toward minus infinity asymptotically. This last result is another illustration that, under deep uncertainty, the asymptotic discount rate is obtained by computing the inequality and precautionary effects as if the worst is certain. The worst in this context is facing an extremely negative trend of economic growth. This result means that one should be willing to invest *at any cost* in any project that generates a sure benefit in the very distant future. This is because there is some probability that the true trend of growth will be negative, such that our collective destiny could well be to go back to the Stone Age. Although this scenario is not certain, and its plausibility may be quite small, the fact that one cannot exclude this scenario forces prudent people under the veil of ignorance to do whatever possible to transfer consumption to the very distant future.

I believe this set of results is crucial to the way we should think about sustainable development. The standard theory of finance fails to recognize the importance of the deep uncertainties that surround the destiny of humanity on this planet. These uncertainties should force our society to reconsider using the standard tools of this theory when evaluating the social benefits and costs of actions aimed at improving the distant future. More specifically, the argument developed in this section suggests using a much lower discount rate to evaluate them. This argument is compatible with using no discounting at all, or even using a negative discount rate, if there is a risk of a regression in our standard of living. This is true even when the probability of such a scenario is small. This result supports a strong interpretation of the precautionary principle.

ON THE FRAGILITY OF THE ASSET PRICING THEORY IN A GAUSSIAN WORLD

Weitzman (2007b) proposes an alternative illustration of the role of deep uncertainties. Suppose, as before, that consumption follows a geometric Brownian motion with a known trend but an unknown volatility. Following the tradition in statistics, Weitzman proposes that our collective beliefs about this unknown volatility can be represented by an inverse gamma distribution, which implies a positive volatility with probability 1. This implies that the unconditional distribution of future consumption has a Student's t-distribution. As before, the ambiguity increases the variance of future consumption. But here, it does much more than that. It generates what statisticians call "fat tails" in the distribution of future consumption. In plain English, although the Student's t-distribution can be made as close to the normal distribution as we want by reducing the uncertainty affecting volatility, this uncertainty dramatically increases the probability of extreme events. It magnifies the precautionary argument so much that the socially desirable discount rate becomes infinitely negative at all maturities.

Although a similar analysis was proposed earlier by Rietz (1988), Weitzman's intriguing result raised much interest in the profession when it was published in 2007. It exposed the fragility of most results in asset pricing theory, which usually assume a Gaussian world. Weitzman has in fact demonstrated that replacing the normal distribution with an arbitrarily close Student's t-distribution to describe macroeconomic uncertainty radically transforms the standard results of the theory.

This result should also make us suspicious of another core assumption in asset pricing theory: that the marginal utility of consumption has a constant elasticity γ, so that

$u'(c) = c^{-\gamma}$. This implies that marginal utility goes to infinity when consumption goes to zero. At the margin, if there is a person whose consumption is infinitely close to zero, we should be willing to increase it at any cost. To illustrate, let's compare two societies. In the first society, all agents consume x, except for one person who consumes 0. In the second society, everyone consumes $\varepsilon > 0$. Under the standard assumption of a constant elasticity of marginal utility, one should always prefer the second society, even when ε tends toward but is not zero. But this does not represent the preferences of an impartial person under the veil of ignorance. Think, for example, about how people value their own mortality risk. If we define death as zero consumption, we observe that people are not willing to sacrifice their entire wealth to reduce their mortality risk. As we saw in chapter 2, the value of statistical life is finite, so marginal utility cannot tend toward infinity.

This argument justifies modifying the shape of the marginal utility function at low consumption levels and revising all asymptotic results in which discount rates are unbounded. However, the finance profession is very reluctant to give up the assumption of a constant elasticity of consumption—an assumption that has the attractive feature of making the equilibrium interest rate independent of the absolute level of economic development, and so determined only by growth expectations rather than the initial condition. This is in line with the observation that interest rates have no historical trend. So the debate about whether to abandon this assumption is still up in the air.

FAT TAILS AND BLACK SWANS

The recent macroeconomic crisis had dramatic effects in many countries. The Greek income per capita shrank by almost 30 percent during the seven-year period from 2008 to 2014 and by approximately 10 percent in Finland, Italy, Spain, and Ireland. A side effect of these macroeconomic catastrophes has been to increase economists' interest in rare events and fat tails. All Gaussian distributions share the same property: Ninety-five percent of events lie in an interval bounded by the mean minus and plus 1.96 times the standard deviation. The magic of the Gaussian world is our ability to determine the probability of any event with only these two parameters—the mean and the standard deviation—which are relatively easy to estimate. But our world is not always Gaussian. For example, if one assumes that the growth rate of the Greek economy is normally distributed and serially uncorrelated, and if we estimate its mean (1.5 percent) and standard deviation (4.3 percent) by using the sample of growth rates between 1969 and 2014, the 30 percent drop in income per capita over a period of seven consecutive years should happen, on average, only once every thirty-six thousand years!

This raises doubt about the realism of the benchmark model presented earlier in which the consumption per capita follows a Brownian motion, and in which growth rates are normally distributed. Instead, the empirical tails of the distribution seem much thicker, with extreme events occurring much more frequently than predicted under normal assumptions.

But if we give up such assumptions, how should one measure the probability of the tails of the distribution of growth? This is a very tricky question since, as I have shown in the previous section, their shape plays a critical role in how we determine our intergenerational responsibilities. If we want to determine the probability of a rare macroeconomic catastrophe that we believe should occur at a secular frequency, using growth data that cover only one or two centuries will not be very helpful. This leaves us with deep uncertainties about the true probabilities of catastrophic events.

Barro (2006, 2009) has proposed an elegant solution to this problem. He proposes that all nations face the same probability of an extreme event, which is defined as a drop in GDP per capita of 15 percent or more. If this is true, then we can learn from disasters that happened around the world throughout the last century to infer the annual probability of disaster for the U.S. economy. Examining thirty-five countries over one hundred years, Barro documented sixty catastrophes, from Germany's 64 percent drop in GDP per capita at the end of World War II, to Spain's 31 percent contraction during the Spanish Civil War, to Argentina's 21 percent contraction during its monetary crisis from 1998 to 2002. This implies a best estimate of the annual probability of a macroeconomic catastrophe of $60 \div (35 \times 100) \approx 1.7\%$. Barro also estimates that the mean contraction in cases of catastrophe is 29 percent.

Although such extreme economic catastrophes have never happened in the United States, they could plausibly occur in the future. Following Martin (2013), let's represent our beliefs about the future of the U.S. economy as follows.

Every year in the business-as-usual scenario, the growth rate is randomly selected from a normal distribution with mean 2.5 percent and volatility 2 percent. But with a probability of 1.7 percent, the growth rate is catastrophic, with a mean of −39 percent and a standard deviation of 25 percent. This risk of disaster should reduce the discount rate, since it weakens the inequality effect and reinforces the precautionary effect. If we use a degree of inequality aversion of 2, these beliefs are compatible with a risk-free discount rate of 2 percent for all maturities.

But note that Barro's model overplays the scientific quantification of our beliefs, because it assumes full knowledge of all its parameters. In particular, it's hard to accept that we have perfect knowledge about the 1.7 percent annual probability of disaster. Barro's sample of thirty-five countries over one hundred years isn't large enough to estimate this probability with precision. In Gollier (2016), I approached this deep uncertainty by using a Bayesian approach with an uninformative prior. This yields a posterior beta distribution for the disaster probability, with a mean of 1.7 percent and a standard deviation of 0.22 percent. I showed that, as is necessarily the case with deep uncertainties, the term structure of socially desirable discount rates decreases. For short and medium time horizons, the discount rates remain close to 2 percent. (In fact, as noted by Collin-Dufresne, Johannes, and Lochstoer [2016], the learning process for disaster probability is very slow, so that parameter uncertainty has a limited impact for small maturities.) But discount rates decrease with maturities and so could become negative for maturities longer than 1,800 years. For extremely long maturities counted in the tens of thousands of years, the discount rate converges asymptotically down to −90 percent. Notice that this is the discount rate that one should use at all maturities if the worst is certain—that is, if the probability of disaster is always 1. But because there is no safe asset or action yielding sure benefits for those maturities, this purpose of this result is primarily theoretical interest.

THE ZERO LOWER BOUND

To sum up, deep uncertainties about long-term growth and fat tails may justify using a low risk-free discount rate. Could this rate even be negative?

Macroeconomists have long believed that the nominal interest rate can never be negative because, if it were, people would immediately withdraw their cash from the bank. But recent episodes following the 2008 financial crisis show that this is not the case. Also, if we account for inflation, the real interest rate can also be negative—and it has been in many countries for extended periods during the last century. There is no normative ground for rejecting a negative discount rate; after all, if we believe the future will be worse than the present, inequality aversion should encourage us to transfer consumption to the future even with a negative return.

Samuelson (1970) justified a zero lower bound for the real discount rate as follows:

In a world of perfect certainty, it is hard to see how people could ever save enough to bring the net productivity of capital all the way down to a zero interest rate. As long as there is a single hilly railroad track left, it would pay at a zero rate of interest to make it level. Why? Because in enough years, the savings in fuel would pay for the cost.

However, this argument implicitly makes the assumption that the benefit of leveling the railway track is permanent and certain. This is not likely to be the case. Aqueducts built by the Romans became useless after some time, either because people left the area, or because new technologies were developed to bring water to the city. Samuelson (1970) recognized this in a footnote: "Before you have recovered the cost of leveling the roadbed of the railway, airplanes might make railways obsolete—or earthquakes might undo your work." In the next chapter, I will examine how to take into account the riskiness of future benefits in cost–benefit analysis.

ECOLOGICAL DISCOUNTING

So far in this chapter, I have described a methodology and its applications for valuing a temporal transfer of consumption. This is useful for evaluating actions that indeed bring some purchasing power through time, such as financial savings and investments. But many of our actions today bring nonfinancial benefits for future generations: improved air or water quality, longer life expectancies, more nonrenewable natural resources, and more biodiversity, for example.

In chapter 2, I explained how to monetize these multidimensional benefits. To evaluate an action that yields an immediate monetary cost and an improvement in air quality in a century, for example, you would perform a two-step cost–benefit analysis. First, ask how future generations would value the nonmonetary impact. Second, discount this value to estimate its present value. The problem with this classic approach is that it is uncertain what value future generations will attach to environmental assets, biodiversity, or air quality. In particular, these values are inherently dependent on the economic circumstances of these generations.

Take, for example, the value of statistical life. Many of the benefits of fighting climate change today take the form of a reduction of the mortality risk of future generations. In the previous section, I explained how the value of statistical life increases with income, since people value a reduction of mortality risk more as they become wealthier. This is why the value of statistical life is greater in the United States than in Bangladesh. The same argument should be used prospectively. In a growing economy, future generations will have a greater value of statistical life than ours; that is, a statistical life will have more value in fifty years than it does today.

Does this mean we should prefer to save one life in fifty years rather than one life today? Not necessarily. Under the veil of ignorance, what matters is the discounted value of statistical life. Suppose that income per capita will double in fifty years; a value of statistical life of $5 million today implies a value of statistical life of $10 million in fifty years. Suppose further that, as assumed in chapter 2, the income elasticity of the value of statistical life is 1, so that the value of statistical life will also double in fifty years. With an inequality aversion of 2, we also know that four units of consumption in fifty years is equivalent to one unit of consumption today. This implies that the present value of the value of statistical life in fifty years is only $2.5 million—and that one should therefore prefer saving a statistical life today (creating a value of $5 million) over saving a statistical life in fifty years.

This illustration suggests a simple way to proceed in the cost–benefit analysis. We prefer saving lives now to saving lives in the future because we are averse to inequalities in the quality and duration of life. But if we assume that life expectancy and quality increase with time, we should be willing to transfer one year of life from the current generation to a future generation. This is exactly the same basic inequality argument for why we discount changes in consumption at a positive rate in a growing economy.

In the same spirit, Guesnerie (2004) and Gollier (2010) have proposed bypassing the two-stage cost–benefit analysis process in which future nonmonetary impacts are first monetized and then discounted, instead defining different discount rates to use to directly discount sure nonmonetary impacts into present equivalents. In a growing economy, growth in the availability of economic and noneconomic goods does not progress at a steady rate. Take for example the case of environmental quality. If we believe that environmental quality will deteriorate in the future, the standard inequality aversion argument implies that we should use a negative "ecological" discount rate to evaluate the future environmental impacts of our green policies today. Uncertainty regarding the quality of the environment in the future reduces this negative discount rate even further. In fact, we can duplicate the entire analysis presented in this chapter for monetized impacts for any nonmonetized impacts. Both the inequality effect and the precautionary effect will differ by type of impact, either because our beliefs about their growth and risk are different or because our attitude toward intergenerational inequalities in these determinants of well-being are heterogeneous.

This provides a strong argument to use a much lower—sometimes even a negative—rate to discount the nonmonetary impacts of our actions today, in particular those impacts that limit the anticipated deterioration of some determinant of our well-being, such as the environment. Finance experts may find this recommendation shocking, being accustomed to the idea that there should be only one discount rate: "the" discount rate. But having different rates is perfectly kosher. The ecological discount rate is just a shortcut to discounting a flow of impacts whose value increases with time. Fossil fuels are the best example of this. Hotelling's rule tells us that because the scarcity of fossil fuels will increase in the future, the value of fossil fuels should increase at a rate exactly equal to the discount rate. Discounting a flow of benefits whose value increases at a rate equaling the discount rate is equivalent to using a zero discount rate. In other words, one should use a zero ecological discount rate to value fossil fuels, together with any other nonrenewable resources for which Hotelling's rule applies. Unsurprisingly, this tells us that one should be indifferent to transferring fossil fuel consumption at the margin along the optimal consumption path. This observation is, in fact, a simple way to justify Hotelling's rule.

LONG-TERMISM AND FINANCIAL MARKETS

I explained earlier why one should measure the degree of individual long-termism induced by financial markets by the equilibrium interest rate that prevails on those markets. The relatively low interest rates observed during the last century suggest that markets induce people to be rather long-termist, at least with respect to risk-free investments. Another standard critique of financial liberalism comes from the high frequency of the financial reports that companies are required to provide to investors. Listed companies typically have to produce these reports on a quarterly basis. This frequent reporting is useful for limiting asymmetric information and insider trading. But opponents to financial liberalism claim that this induces managers to become too focused on the short-term performance of their companies to the detriment of actions favorable to their long-term performance. This is a misunderstanding, as I will show now.

To illustrate the argument in its simplest form, suppose that aggregate consumption follows a geometric Brownian motion, such that the equilibrium interest rate r is independent of maturity and is constant through time. Suppose that financial reporting must be made on a yearly basis. Consider a manager who contemplates the possibility of investing in a project that costs 1 today and will generate a single cash flow b in $t > 1$ years. Let's also suppose that b is greater than $\exp(rt)$, so that the project has a positive net present value and is therefore socially desirable. As the story goes, the problem is that this benefit will materialize in many years, but the loan must be made now to finance the project.

Next year, when markets will swallow the next annual report, they will observe that the firm is now more indebted, with no additional revenue. The new debt amounts to $D = \exp(rt)$. Anticipating the negative reaction of the market, the manager of the firm would therefore prefer not to invest in this long-term project, inducing short-termism.

This argument is wrong because it fails to recognize that the company will be endowed next year with a new asset. This asset corresponds to the ownership of an investment that will generate cash flow b in $t - 1$ years. If this investment is liquid, it could be sold on markets at a price equal to the discounted value $B = b \times \exp(-r(t-1))$ of this future benefit. So, the balance sheet of the company next year will contain, at the same time, a new debt amounting to D and a new asset whose fair value is B. In net, the market value of the firm will be increased next year by the decision to invest this year if, and only if, B is greater than D. It is important to check that this is equivalent to requiring that b is larger than $\exp(rt)$, which is the social desirability condition that we assumed from the beginning. Thus, although the project will generate a cash flow only in the distant future, a manager concerned only with the value of the firm next year will be incentivized to implement it. The frequency of reporting does not influence the decision to invest. Only the interest rate will.

This argument can also be used in an intergenerational context. Each generation can be interested in investing in projects whose cash flows will primarily benefit generations living in the distant future. Think, for example, about improving your house. One of the benefits of doing so is of course to benefit from a more comfortable home. But another benefit comes from the ability to sell your house at a higher price later on in your life. The increased price arguably measures the present value of the flow of the additional monetary benefits of the greater comfort enjoyed by the next owner. Because this next owner can anticipate to sell the house at an even higher price to someone in the next generation, the price that this next owner will be willing to pay will, in fact, correspond to the discounted incremental benefit of the renovation enjoyed by all future generations of owners.

A key element of this argument is the ability of the owner of the investment to sell it to other investors at any time in the future. This requires the new asset created by the investment to be tradable, or liquid. If a homeowner assumes that their home will be confiscated in the future, they will not be able to appropriate the full benefit of their renovation effort. They will become short-termist. In fact, by making many investments liquid, financial markets induce people to become more long-termist, expanding their vision of the impacts of their own investments beyond their own lives. Of course, this argument is limited by the many frictions that exist on financial markets.

SUMMARY

Do we do too much for future generations? In this chapter, I have tried to answer this challenging question by examining the case of actions that generate sure benefits for future generations. This question can be answered by determining the minimum risk-free rate of return at which one would be willing to act to improve that future. This is the risk-free discount rate. But in a growing economy, investing for the future has the undesirable effect of increasing intergenerational inequalities. This justifies using a positive discount rate. This discount rate increases with the degree of inequality aversion and the anticipated consumption growth rate. If we believe that Western economies will continue to grow forever at approximately 2 percent per year, it is reasonable to use a discount rate of 4 percent per year. This almost completely eliminate impacts that will occur more than two or three decades from our evaluation radar. At a growth rate of 2 percent per annum, consumption per capita doubles every thirty-four years, and is multiplied by a factor of 54 over two centuries. In short, the story goes as follows: Why should we care about people who will be more than fifty times wealthier than us? If this is the correct representation of our collective beliefs about the future, a high discount rate is justified, and our responsibility toward future generations is indeed very limited.

My understanding is that our collective beliefs are very different from the eternally increasing prosperity described earlier. We face potentially diminishing expectations (secular stagnation?) and uncertainty concerning the distant future. Exactly as households sacrifice some present well-being by saving more when their future income becomes more uncertain, we should collectively make more efforts to improve a more uncertain future. In our decentralized economies, this should be done by reducing the discount rate so that more sure investment projects pass the test of a positive net present value.

But by how much should we decrease the discount rate? Well, this critically depends upon the way we calibrate uncertainty. If we use the classic approach in finance and macroeconomics to assume that consumption per capita follows a geometric Brownian motion, the reduction is really marginal. But if we recognize that the long-term growth process is affected by deep uncertainties, fat tails, and potential macroeconomic disasters with an uncertain probability of occurrence, then the impact of uncertainty on the socially desirable discount rate is huge, in particular when considering the evaluation of very distant benefits and costs. One can play with the numbers, but at the end of the day, a relatively clear picture emerges. A rate of around 2 percent should be used to discount risk-free monetary benefits that will materialize within the next three or four decades. But for more distant time horizons, discount rates converging asymptotically on small rates somewhere close to 0 percent should be used.

This means that, contrary to the typical approach of the theory of finance in which prudence plays a minimal role, precaution should be a driving force in judging our collective responsibilities toward future generations, given the intensity of the uncertainties with which they will be confronted. Although this will certainly remain a subject of contention, the very low risk-free real discount rate that we recommend for extra-long maturities results from the idea that, although we have positive expectations for the long-term growth of the economy (meaning that inequality aversion justifies a positive rate), this effect is almost entirely compensated for by the precautionary effect for distant time horizons.

4

IS THE WORLD TOO RISKY?

Life is inherently risky, and the outcome of any action we take is subject to uncertainty. However, some actions entail more risk than others. Since Arrow (1963, 1971), economists have recognized that human beings are risk averse; we prefer an action with a sure benefit to a risky one with the same expected benefit. Earlier in this book, risk aversion justified our assumption of inequality aversion under the veil of ignorance. So, in a standard cost–benefit analysis, we should thus associate riskier actions with a risk penalty when deciding how much risk to accept.

The aggregation of our individual actions leads to a collective risk, which translates into uncertain macroeconomic growth. There are some actions few of us have control over but that have consequences felt by the entire population—consequences crucial to our destiny. For example, the Apollo program and its successors for space exploration will probably be very important for future generations, together with the development of biotechnology, genetic manipulations, nuclear fusion, and the like. Think also about ITER, the international project to use fusion, the nuclear reaction that powers the sun, as an infinitely renewable source of cheap electricity production. Some a priori, somewhat innocuous, decisions, such as to develop Facebook or Amazon or to incentivize economic agents to reduce fossil fuel consumption (e.g., through electric cars, photovoltaic panels, home retrofitting), may also have crucial long-term impacts on our society. But these impacts are all uncertain and risky. In this chapter, I examine how to adapt the evaluation methodology outlined so far to the case of risky projects and risky assets. This will be useful in answering the question raised by the title of this chapter.

During and following the financial crisis of 2008, as in the aftermath of the bust of earlier bubbles, many voices claimed that economic agents such as banks and hedge funds not only accepted bad risks but accepted too much risk. This suggests that there is a socially desirable level of risk in our society. How can we characterize this level of risk? In our day-to-day decisions, what operational rule can we use to enlighten our choices? Did we take too much risk in the past? And, finally, did financial markets incentivize market participants to take too much risk on their own? To answer these questions, we need to determine what risks we can accept that raise social welfare, where social welfare is defined as the unweighted sum of the flow of expected utility enjoyed by future generations who will live on this planet—or elsewhere.

RISK AVERSION

We saw in chapter 1 that if we accept the independence axiom (which has a strong normative appeal), we should recognize that the expected utility of consumption is the best way to represent individual preferences under risk. To simplify the discussion, as in chapter 3, let's suppose that consumption is limited to a single good. This implicitly means that we are able to monetize all nonmonetary benefits in all states of nature, as explained in chapter 2.

The building block of any theory of risk pricing is risk aversion. In the expected utility model, risk aversion is a direct consequence of the assumption that the marginal utility of consumption is decreasing. Consider the case of a person who faces two equally possible states of nature. The situation is risky ex ante because one state yields a larger consumption level than the other. Decreasing marginal utility means that transferring one unit of consumption from the good state to the bad raises expected utility ex ante, as it raises utility in the bad state more than it reduces utility in the good state. Another way to say this is that insurance is socially desirable. Indeed, an actuarially fair insurance contract that promises an indemnity of 2 in the bad state in exchange for an insurance premium of 1 to be paid ex ante will result in the same state-specific change in consumption.

Under risk aversion, any mean-preserving reduction in risk increases welfare. But in general, risk reduction devices have a cost. Insurance usually yields a premium larger than the expected indemnity, and purchasing a less risky portfolio also reduces its expected return. So, to use cost–benefit analysis to determine the efficient choice, we must put a price on risk.

To do this, let's reconsider the problem raised earlier of the person facing two equally likely states of nature. Suppose this person consumes twice as much in the good state than in the bad. If this were you, how much consumption in the good state would you be willing to give up to increase consumption in the bad state by 1? If your answer is 4, your degree of risk aversion is $\gamma = 2$, with a marginal utility of consumption c being $c^{-\gamma}$. As we saw earlier in earlier chapters, and in line with claims by prominent economists on this subject, we will later assume a collective risk aversion of 2. Under the veil of ignorance, risk aversion and inequality aversion are the same notion and should be treated accordingly.

More useful for cost–benefit analysis is the notion of risk premium, which is a monetary valuation of the cost of risk. The risk premium is the reduction in expected consumption that one is willing to pay in exchange for the full elimination of risk. Suppose, for example, that final consumption has an equal probability of being either 100 or 200, and that relative risk aversion γ is 2, so that the utility function is $U(c) = -1/c$. Then, the certainty equivalent consumption is 133.33, because $U(133.33)$ is equal to $0.5U(100) + 0.5U(200)$. Compared to the expected consumption of 150, this is a reduction by 16.67. This measures the risk premium.

A simple rule called the Arrow–Pratt approximation (Arrow 1963, Pratt 1964) states that the risk premium, expressed as a share of expected consumption, for the full elimination of a risk is approximately equal to half the product of risk aversion by the variance of the relative consumption, where relative consumption is the ratio of actual consumption over expected consumption. In the earlier example, expected consumption is 150, and relative consumption is either 2/3 or 4/3, with a variance of 1/9. Thus, the risk premium is approximately 1/9 of expected consumption; that is, 16.67. It happens that the approximation is exact in this numerical example. It can also be shown that the Arrow–Pratt approximation is exact when relative aversion is constant and the risk on the logarithm of consumption is normally distributed.

THE SOCIAL BENEFIT OF MUTUALIZATION, INSURANCE, AND RISK-SHARING

Not many benefits come free in our world. Diversification is one of these rare free gifts and is a simple mechanism to reduce risk.

Say that you and your friend Harris both face the same income risk of earning 100 or 200 with equal probabilities. But you work in the new tech industry and Harris works in the education sector, so your two risks are independent. Suppose that you agree to mutualize your incomes, so that you each get 50 percent of both. If you do this, your final income will be either 100, 150, or 200 with a probability of 1/4 , 1/2 , or 1/4, respectively. Observe that, by accepting this free deal, you have reduced the probability of extreme income without modifying your expected income. As a consequence, the variance of your relative income is now down to 1/18, as is your relative risk premium. Because your risk is smaller, it has a smaller impact on your well-being ex ante (Arrow 1971). This is the benefit of diversification. If your friend Jennifer has the same independent risk profile, you could further reduce your risk by integrating her into your mutual agreement. You, Harris, and Jennifer would all benefit from this. At the limit, by integrating many people with an independent risk profile, the law of large numbers tells us that every member of the risk pool will end up with an almost certain final income of 150. If feasible, this mutual arrangement will create a social value of 11 percent of the members' expected income.

This shows that it's socially desirable to disseminate risks to the largest possible community of citizens. The intuition of this result is based on the Arrow–Pratt approximation, which states that the cost of risk is approximately proportional to its variance, or equivalent to the *square* of its size. This implies that if each of the n people in the community bears $1/n$ of the risk, each bears a cost of risk proportional to $1/n^2$, yielding a collective cost of risk proportional to $n/n^2 = 1/n$. When n tends toward infinity, this risk dissemination washes out the collective cost of risk.

The elimination of diversifiable risks has an important implication for their valuation. Although we are collectively risk averse, we should collectively behave in a risk-neutral way in the face of these risks. This means that we should undertake these risks as soon as their expected return is positive. Limiting our exposure to these risks would just weaken economic growth. This result is often referred to as the Arrow–Lind theorem (Arrow and Lind 1970). This theorem has left many people with the mistaken impression that governments should be risk neutral when evaluating and prioritizing their actions; we will see why this is a mistake later on in the chapter.

Our society has established various mutualization mechanisms that bring benefits to all of us. The family institution is a good example—you and your partner pool your income and so collectively reduce your risk, but even in multigenerational households where more than one person contributes income, its size is limited. Moreover, an event like divorce quickly ends such an arrangement. There are many mechanisms that include far more people; for instance, the social security systems that we see in most advanced countries. Unemployment insurance, life insurance, and life annuities, but also auto and home insurance, all contribute to the elimination of risks that can mostly be diversified through mutualization.

The first formal risk-sharing mechanisms were created by private initiatives. Marine insurance was organized in Genoa in the fourteenth century. Fire and life insurance emerged in London in the seventeenth century. The first shareholding company—a crucial financial innovation that helped investors and entrepreneurs share risks with each other—was the Bazacle Company of Toulouse, founded in 1372 (Le Bris, Goetzmann, and Pouget 2015). The shareholders of this watermill company managed, mutualized, and traded risk continuously until its nationalization in 1946. Today, financial markets provide myriad contractual arrangements for people to better disseminate and share their risks.

SOLIDARITY AND RISK-SHARING DO NOT WORK EFFICIENTLY IN OUR SOCIETY

Various problems limit our ability to get the full economic benefit of mutualization and diversification. First, there may be a commitment problem, as lucky members of the risk pool (i.e., those who get an income of 200 would prefer to leave the pool). The enforceability of social and legal contracts preventing such departures are central to our ability to implement risk-sharing devices eliminating diversifiable risks. Another problem is the reduced incentive for members to reduce risk. If people get full insurance against their underlying risk, they will not naturally exert the effort necessary to limit the probability of a poor outcome. Employees will shirk, insurers will not implement preventive actions, and unemployed people will not search for new jobs. Because the cost of prevention is usually private, whereas most of the benefits go to the other members of the pool, the mutual institution would have to fight against this moral hazard of reduced risk prevention. This may be so costly that it ends up being better to leave people alone to bear individual risk. Moreover, if the risk characteristic of individual profiles is private information, only the riskiest profiles will want to join the pool. This adverse selection problem is another source of inefficiency in the sharing of risk. Adverse selection and moral hazard are sources of market inefficiency and failure under asymmetric information; that is, when some stakeholders to a contract have better information than others (e.g., regarding the effort exerted by some of them or the risk type of the collective action). Indeed, economic theory underwent a paradigmatic revolution over the last four decades as economists realized how difficult it is to transfer and disseminate private information in our society. The works of my colleagues Jean-Jacques Laffont and Jean Tirole in Toulouse have been widely recognized as pioneering in this domain (see, for example, Laffont and Tirole 1993). Bengt Holmström, Eric Maskin, Paul Milgrom, Michael Spence, Joseph Stiglitz, and Richard Zeckhauser are the other big names who founded so-called contract theory.

A moral hazard problem inherent to any risk transfer scheme under asymmetric information comes from the limited incentive of the originator of the risk to manage and control it. This problem has been identified as the main source of the subprime crisis. The original lenders usually did not retain the credit risks associated with the mortgages they underwrote. Because the final risk-bearers did not correctly value and price the risks they accepted, the originators of the credit risk had no incentive to correctly select and monitor them. As a result, socially undesirable risks were undertaken at an unprecedented scale.

The market inefficiencies associated with moral hazard and adverse selection are huge. It leaves smaller businesses to bear their own risk, thereby inhibiting investment, recruitment, and growth. In such cases, diversifiable risk should not be priced risk neutrally, as suggested by the Arrow–Lind theorem. Rather, we should value the benefit of economic policies aimed at improving risk-sharing in the economy.

Shiller (2003) rightly claims that much remains to be done to better insure individual risks that are diversifiable through mutualization and suggests that the digital revolution will help us do that by reducing the cost of acquiring and processing information to fight moral hazard and adverse selection. Better insuring unemployment, idiosyncratic longevity risk, or the risk affecting the market value of houses (which is usually the household's main asset) is certainly an ambitious but achievable collective objective.

PENALIZING ACTIONS THAT INCREASE COLLECTIVE RISK

Earlier I made the simplifying assumption that individual risks are not correlated with each other—your income faces totally separate risks from Harris's. This is a critical assumption when applying the law of large numbers. Indeed, its risk-sharing application implies that the mutualization of individual risks washes them out completely. But suppose, alternatively, that individual risks are impacted by one or more common factors. The simplest one to imagine is economic growth itself. An improvement in the economy is good news for most people's incomes, as for most investments' social return; in a downturn, the reverse is true. Clearly, mutualizing risks will not eliminate the global risk coming from a common factor like economic growth. This limits the creation of value generated by the mutual arrangement.

If individual risks were diversifiable, consumption per capita would be certain. In reality, consumption per capita fluctuates over time in a random way. We already examined quite extensively the implications of this macroeconomic uncertainty for the selection of the risk-free discount rate. We now examine its implication for the evaluation of actions whose benefits are statistically linked to aggregate consumption—that is, whose risk is undiversifiable. As explained in the introduction to this chapter, this raises the question of the acceptability and efficiency of the collective risk.

Under risk aversion, collective risk is undesirable if it is not compensated by a large expected return, because it cannot be diversified away. Consider a costly action today that yields some social benefit per capita b_t at some future date t. This social benefit can be statistically related to consumption per capita c_t. How should we price this uncertain benefit? We hereafter assume that risk-sharing mechanisms efficiently disseminate the risk associated with this action to the entire population, so that everyone bears the same benefit b_t from this action. Remember that marginal utility measures how much utility increases when consumption increases by 1. Now, this action increases future consumption by b_t, so that future utility is increased by $b_t U'(c_t)$. This utility benefit is uncertain, so we should measure the future impact of this action by its expected value $E b_t U'(c_t)$. In order to transform this utility gain into present consumption units, we divide the expected utility gain by the current marginal utility of consumption. Thus, the present value of the future uncertain benefit is measured by $Eb_t U'(c_t) / U'(c_0)$. It is the sure immediate benefit per capita that has the same impact on the utilitarian inter-generational welfare as the uncertain future benefit b_t. It should therefore be compared to the immediate cost of the action to determine whether the action improves inter-generational welfare.

For example, suppose that we collectively believe that in thirty years, there will be an equal probability of consumption per capita either doubling or remaining as it is today. Let's say there's an investment project that will generate $4 in expectation in thirty years for each dollar invested today. Consider three different projects that satisfy this condition. In project S (safe), $4 will be obtained with certainty, independent of the realized growth of the economy. In project G (good state), a benefit of $8 will be obtained in the good state, but the project completely fails in the bad state. Finally, in project B (bad state), $8 will be obtained in the bad state, but nothing will be obtained in the good state. How should we rank these three projects? The best project is project B, because it delivers more consumption when it is the most valuable; that is, in the bad state. Project G is the worst project, because it fails in that state. In fact, when relative risk aversion γ is 2, the risk-adjusted net present value of projects B, S, and G are respectively equal to $3, $1.50, and $0 per dollar invested today.

The simplest case arises when the future benefit of the action is statistically independent from future consumption, as is the case in project S. Because the expectation of the product of two independent random variables is equal to the product of their expectation, the present value of the future benefit is equal to $Eb_t[EU'(c_t)/U'(c_0)]$. Remember that the bracketed term in this expression is the discount factor to be used to discount safe benefits. The Arrow–Lind theorem applies in this case. At the margin, risk aversion is a second-order phenomenon. The mutualization of the risk in the population makes everyone bear an infinitesimally small fraction of it, at no marginal cost.

Suppose, alternatively, that the future benefit of the action is positively correlated with future consumption, as is the case in project G. Obviously, implementing this action increases the collective risk. The decreasing marginal utility implies that larger benefits go with smaller marginal utility. The action is thus less attractive than in the independent case, because more benefits materialize when they are less valued. This implies that $Eb_t U'(c_t)/U'(c_0)$ is less than $Eb_t EU'(c_t)/U'(c_0)$, which is the present value of the expected future benefit discounted at the risk-free rate. We see that this procedure penalizes actions that raise the collective risk by reducing their net present value.

Symmetric to this are actions whose future benefits are negatively correlated with future consumption, as in project B. These actions dampen negative shocks to the economy by generating relatively more benefits in these circumstances. In other words, these actions hedge the collective risk. This should be positively evaluated when measuring the impact of an action on welfare. The present value of the future benefit is greater than the expected benefit discounted at the risk-free discount rate, thereby imbedding the value of insurance into the evaluation procedure.

BACK TO THE BROWNIAN WORLD:
THE CONSUMPTION-BASED CAPITAL
ASSET PRICING MODEL

Let's now translate these ideas into simple operational rules. As in the other parts of this book, I'm interested in describing decision rules that show whether our actions are aligned with our collective aspirations. As in the benchmark case examined in chapter 3, suppose that inequality aversion γ is constant and that consumption follows a geometric Brownian motion, such that log consumption at time t is normally distributed with mean μt and variance $\sigma^2 t$. Finally, suppose that future benefit is statistically linked to future consumption in the following way: When consumption increases by 1 percent, benefit increases by β percent in expectation, where β is a known constant. (Independent risk should not be priced, as it will be eliminated through mutualization, so adding white noise to the picture won't change anything.) Observe that β is a simple measure of the statistical relationship between the social benefit of an action (including all externalities) and consumption. It's a measure of an action's contribution to collective risk and is often referred to as the socioeconomic beta (or consumption capital asset pricing model [CCAPM] beta) of a project.

I show in the technical appendix that, for investment projects with such a risk profile, the investment decision rule that is compatible with the public good is to implement this type of project if, and only if, its expected benefit discounted at a risk-adjusted rate is positive. The risk adjustment is obtained by adding to the risk-free rate characterized in chapter 3 as risk premium $\beta\pi$, which is proportional to the socio-economic beta of a project. The systematic risk premium $\pi = \gamma\sigma^2$ is the risk premium associated with a risk profile equivalent to the risk of aggregate consumption ($\beta = 1$). This systematic risk premium is equal to the product of the coefficient of inequality aversion by the variance of the consumption growth rate.

To sum up, the riskiness of future benefit is integrated into the evaluation procedure by risk-adjusting the rate at which the expected benefit is discounted. If an action raises collective risk—that is, if its beta is positive—the risk-adjusted discount rate is higher than the risk-free rate, thereby reducing its net present value. On the contrary, if an action hedges collective risk—that is, if its beta is negative—then the risk-adjusted discount rate is lower than the risk-free rate, implying a greater net present value. A greater contribution to collective risk implies a higher risk-adjusted discount rate, and a smaller social value for the action. The systematic risk premium π quantifies the penalty that should be imposed on riskier projects. This variable plays a critical role in determining how much risk economic agents should accept. It measures at the same time the minimum compensation required to compensate people for the increased risk they will have to bear and the additional cost of capital imposed on firms that implement risky investments. Remember that the discount rate is the minimum internal rate of return that makes an investment project socially desirable. The fact that the discount rate is adjusted for risk means that riskier projects (i.e., those with a higher socioeconomic beta) require a higher minimum internal rate of return to make them socially desirable.

ARE WE TOO CONSERVATIVE IN OUR COLLECTIVE RISK-TAKING BEHAVIOR?

The macroeconomic risk premium $\pi = \gamma\sigma^2$ is the price of risk in the Brownian world. It is the increase in the discount rate to be used to evaluate a project with a unit beta; that is, a project whose future benefit increases by 1 percent in expectation when consumption increases by 1 percent. Because final consumption per capita is the aggregation of all actions made by economic agents, such a unit-beta project is the "average" risk profile of all actions undertaken in the economy.

One can estimate this average risk profile by measuring the volatility σ of past consumption growth rates. In chapter 3, using historical data from the Western world, we took $\sigma = 3\%$ per year. Assuming $\gamma = 2$ implies a macroeconomic risk premium of $\pi = 2 \times (3\%)^2 \approx 0.2\%$. In the Brownian world, safe projects should be discounted at 3.8 percent as seen in the previous chapter, whereas risky projects with a risk profile representative of the economy should be discounted at a rate of 3.8 + 0.2 = 4 percent. This is usually considered a very small risk premium. If this was the recommendation for evaluating risky projects in our economy, it would induce much more risk-taking than we see today.

Investors and entrepreneurs are incentivized to take risk in our decentralized economy because the price of risk is positive. The simplest way to see this is to measure the extra return investors have obtained on financial markets by purchasing a riskier portfolio. Table 4.1 shows the return of a diversified portfolio of equity in different countries over various periods of time. In the short run, investors

Table 4.1 Real Return on a Diversified Equity Portfolio (annualized, in percent)

	2000–2014	1965–2014	1900–2014
China	3.0		
France	0.6	5.2	3.2
Germany	1.5	5.0	3.2
Japan	0.1	4.4	4.1
United Kingdom	1.0	6.2	5.3
United States	2.4	3.4	6.5
World	1.8	5.3	5.2

Source: Dimson, Marsh, and Staunton 2015.

who purchased such a portfolio took much more risk than people who invested in sovereign short-term bonds, which are the safest assets on financial markets. Such investors were compensated for bearing this macroeconomic risk by enjoying an annualized rate of return of 6.5 percent on their investments. On the other side of the market, this forced risky shareholding companies to deliver large dividends, yielding a large cost of capital.

In Table 4.2, I compute the equity premium for these different countries by subtracting the rate of return of the safest assets from the equity return. In the United States over the longest time period, from 1900 to the end of 2014, the equity premium was 4.4 percent per year. A diversified portfolio of equity is typically leveraged because firms also finance their investment through debt. It is generally assumed that the CCAPM beta of a diversified portfolio of equities is around $\beta = 3$: A 1 percent increase in aggregate consumption

Table 4.2 Equity Premium (annualized, in percent)

	2000–2014	1965–2014	1900–2014
China	2.3		
France	0.1	4.5	6.0
Germany	1.0	3.3	5.6
Japan	0.0	4.1	6.0
United Kingdom	0.9	4.8	4.4
United States	2.8	2.5	5.6
World	2.2	4.4	4.3

Source: Dimson, Marsh and Staunton 2015.

increases the market value of such a portfolio by 3 percent on average (Bansal and Yaron 2004). This implies that the consumption-based CAPM model predicts an equity premium of around $3\pi = 0.6\%$. This should be compared to the equity premium of 5.6 percent observed in the United States during the period from 1900 to 2014. The discrepancy between these two risk premiums is usually referred to as the "equity premium puzzle." It states that financial markets seem to be much more risk averse than socially desirable, disproportionally increasing the cost of capital of riskier firms, thus inhibiting them from investing, recruiting, and innovating. Raising the rate at which they are incentivized by markets to discount their future cash flows induces them to be short-termist. This is a reversal compared to what we said about safe projects in the Brownian world. Because the socially desirable risk-free rate of 3.8 percent was higher than the observed interest rate on markets, we claimed that markets were too long-termist for risk-free investment projects. The opposite is true for risky ones.

The short-termism of financial markets has often been criticized, sometimes with exaggeration. For example, it is often claimed that hedge funds force companies they hold to generate a return of at least 15 percent per year. This is clearly not what historical data on returns of traded equity tells us actually happens, since the average return of equity has been a much smaller 6.5 percent per year in the United States over the last century. And there is no reason that, at equilibrium, private equity delivers a better outcome net of managerial costs. But the critiques of financial markets are right to claim that a real equity return of 6.5 percent per year is too large to be compatible with the common good. This return imposes a large cost of capital for entrepreneurs, which tends to limit their investments, economic growth, employment, and welfare. There are risky investment projects that many households would be willing to finance given their risk and time preferences, but financial markets are unable to bring the two parties (savers and entrepreneurs) of this mutually advantageous trade together.

To sum up, this analysis suggests that it is socially desirable to be much less conservative than markets in the treatment of risk when evaluating public and private actions. If our premises here are correct, the price of risk should be reduced, implying more incentive to take risk in the economy. We should invest in projects with more uncertain collective outcomes in exchange for larger expected returns. The bottom line is that one should accept living in a riskier but more prosperous world. This is the verdict of the

Brownian case, in which the jury evaluates the merit of different financial systems by using the criterion of a utilitarian social welfare function.

THE "CONJOINED TRIPLET": AVERSION TO INEQUALITY, RISK, AND INTERTEMPORAL FLUCTUATIONS

Modeling economic growth with a Brownian motion leads to a risk-free rate that is too high and a risk premium that is too small. Could we solve these two problems by modifying our coefficient γ? The short answer is no. Under discounted expected utility, the degree γ of concavity of the utility function plays two different roles: risk aversion and inequality aversion. Reducing it will reduce the risk-free rate, which solves the risk-free rate puzzle, but it will also reduce the risk premium, which makes the equity premium even worse. A simple idea would be to disentangle inequality aversion from risk aversion.

Selden (1978) and Epstein and Zin (1991) have proposed an alternative decision model to do just this. Their model focuses on a single individual who can transfer their own consumption across time and states of nature, but the same idea can be applied when the transfer in time is in favor of another generation. Their "recursive preferences" model uses a risk-utility function to estimate the future certainty equivalent consumption and a time-utility function to measure the welfare benefit of reducing intergenerational inequalities. This recursive model may better explain how people actually behave, but like Harsanyi (1955) and Broome (1991), I strongly object to its normative usefulness. There is just no moral justification for differentiating risk attitudes under the veil of ignorance.

Broome (1991) examined the way in which goods "located" in each of three "dimensions"—time, people, and states of nature—make up overall goodness, arguing these dimensions are linked by the independence axiom that supports what he calls the interpersonal addition theorem. The utilitarian welfare function derived from this adds up utils across different periods of time, agents, and states of nature. This triple summation operation implies that, under the veil of ignorance, the concavity of the utility function U represents, at the same time, inequality aversion, risk aversion, and aversion to intertemporal consumption fluctuations. These three concepts make up a "conjoined triplet." Suppose we are indifferent about a leaky transfer in which $4 is taken from person X to give $1 to person Y and person Y consumes half what person X consumes. In other words, this is exactly what we would be willing to do under the veil of ignorance, assuming that we face the same chance of becoming either person X or person Y in the future. Therefore, it is also true that when we face some uncertainty about two equally likely states X and Y, in which we would consume twice as much in state X as in state Y, we would be willing to give up as much as $4 in state X to get $1 more in state Y.

Following Barsky et al. (1997), Atkinson et al. (2009) investigated this question by surveying more than three thousand people's attitudes to risk, income inequality over space, and income inequality over time and arrived at a median value of risk aversion in the range of 3 to 5. People typically rejected a policy that gave equal chances of doubling income or reducing it by one-quarter, but they accepted a policy in which the reduction amounted to 15 percent. At the same time, the median value of inequality aversion was in the range of 2 to 3. The proximity of these two estimations is good news, since it suggests that people use the same utilitarian method to make choices under risk and under inequality. However, the same study also generated a greater value for aversion to consumption fluctuations over time. The authors also found a weakly positive correlation among the three measures of the concavity of the utility function.

The more recent literature on long-run risks initiated by Bansal and Yaron provides interesting arguments for using a degree of risk aversion of around 10 and a degree of aversion to consumption fluctuations somewhere between 0.5 and 1. In particular, proponents of this literature have demonstrated that the risk-free rate puzzle and the equity premium puzzle can be explained by using this calibration of recursive preferences together with the existence of some predictability about the trend and volatility of the future consumption growth rate. I have two reservations about their arguments, however. First, a relative risk aversion of 10 is outrageously large and unrealistic. Second, when these recursive preferences are used in an intergenerational context, the parameter they call aversion to consumption fluctuations over time must in fact be reinterpreted as inequality aversion. I personally believe that an inequality aversion below 1 is incompatible with our collective preferences; that is, that inequality aversion should instead be around 2. But this remains an ethical question that should be addressed by society as a whole, not by an obscure community of experts.

ARE WE REALLY COLLECTIVELY SO RISK AVERSE?

In the previous chapter, I expressed some reservations about how realistically the Brownian assumption describes macroeconomic uncertainty, in particular when considering actions with long-lasting impacts on the economy and the environment. These critiques had a common characteristic: They all suggest that the Brownian assumption underestimates uncertainty. If one underestimates the risk affecting future consumption per capita, one also underestimates the risk of all investment projects with which it is positively correlated. This implies that the cost of risk is underestimated. Maybe markets are right, after all, to impose such a large equity premium. In fact, the jury is still out. Let's review a few arguments for this.

We saw in chapter 3 that the thickness of the tails of the economy's annual growth rate distribution plays a crucial role in determining the risk-free discount rate. It's no surprise that it also plays a crucial role in determining the macroeconomic risk premium. In the Brownian world, it is equal to $\gamma\sigma^2$, where σ is the standard deviation of the growth rate, which is normally distributed. Following Rietz (1988) and Weitzman (2007b), let's assume alternatively that the growth rate of consumption has a Student's t-distribution, assuming the same standard deviation and degree of freedom, such that the two density functions are almost the same, but with the Student's t-distribution having fatter tails. In such a case, the macroeconomic risk premium goes to plus infinity. If this describes our collective beliefs, we should be infinitely risk averse. In other words, we should invest only in perfectly safe projects! This reverses the equity premium puzzle, with markets now being too lax on risk-taking.

Of course, this result is of limited practical use given its extreme final recommendation. A more operational approach has been proposed by Barro (2006, 2009), who has attempted to quantify a rational way to build our beliefs about the frequency of catastrophic events. As explained in chapter 3, Barro used the observed frequency of macroeconomic catastrophes in thirty-five countries over one hundred years to build a compound probability distribution of the annual growth rate of consumption. Following Martin (2013), this leads to an assumption of two regimes. In these regimes, the growth rate is normally distributed. In the business-as-usual regime, the expected growth rate is 2.5 percent, and the standard deviation 2 percent. In the catastrophic regime, the expected growth rate is −39 percent, and the standard deviation is 25 percent. Every year, the probability of the catastrophic regime is 1.7 percent. In this context, the macroeconomic risk premium increases to 1.3 percent. This is higher than the initial $\pi = 0.2\%$ computed in the previous section but still far below the equity premium observed on financial markets during the last century.

An alternative approach is to recognize that the growth process is affected by deep uncertainties. Suppose, for example, that we collectively believe that the growth process is

Brownian and that the trend of growth, although constant, is uncertain. I explained in chapter 3 that although this doesn't affect the measure of short-term macroeconomic risk much, the uncertainty does have an enormous impact on long-run uncertainty. This implies that the macroeconomic risk premium should have an increasing term structure. In Gollier (2008), I assumed growth volatility was σ and that our belief about this trend was normally distributed with mean μ_0 and standard deviation σ_0, a parameter that measures the ambiguity affecting growth probabilities. In this case, c_t is log-normally distributed with mean μt and variance $(\sigma^2 + \sigma_0^2 t)t$. This shows that the variance of consumption, which was measured by σ^2 in the Brownian case, must now be replaced by $\sigma^2 + \sigma_0^2 t$. This means, in particular, that the macroeconomic risk premium, which used to be $\gamma\sigma^2$, is now equal to $\pi_t = \sigma^2 + \sigma_0^2 t$. The macroeconomic risk premium increases linearly with maturity.

To measure this effect, suppose, for example, that the uncertainty about the trend is given by a mean of 2 percent and a standard deviation of 1 percent, such that there is a 95 percent probability that the true trend of growth is somewhere between 0 percent and 4 percent. In this case, the macroeconomic risk premium increases by 1 percent for every fifty years of additional maturity.

The unboundedness of the asymptotic value of the risk premium comes from the normality assumption about the true trend of the economy. One cannot exclude the plausibility that the true trend is deep in the negative and positive domains, implying an unbounded uncertainty about the real economic outcome of very distant future generations.

This should induce us to be particularly reluctant to take actions that increases the uncertainty further. On the contrary, we should greatly value any action that hedges this enormous collective long-term risk. This is precisely what a large macroeconomic risk premium does.

One should also recognize that other parameters governing the growth process are also deeply uncertain, such as the volatility, or the frequency of extreme macroeconomic events. Introducing these additional elements into the calibration of our collective beliefs magnifies the long-term macroeconomic risk and consequently raises the long-term macroeconomic risk premium (Gollier 2016).

MY NORMATIVE CAPITAL ASSET PRICING THEORY

Normative theories are useful in providing arguments both for and against various principles to drive collective actions. However, at the end of the day, operational rules must be decided. Here is what I propose. Suppose that we agree on the following two normative foundations of our collective actions:

> *Collective aspiration*: Our collective goal is to implement any action that raises intergenerational welfare, which is the sum of the successive generational expected utilities. Imbedded in this goal is a collective aversion to a consumption inequality of 2, meaning that one should be willing to sacrifice at most 4 consumption units from a

wealthy person to deliver one unit of consumption more to a poor person whose consumption level is half that enjoyed by the wealthy person.

Collective beliefs: The growth rate process is a random walk. In the absence of catastrophe, the annual growth rate is normally distributed with a standard deviation of 2 percent. There is some deep uncertainty about the expected growth rate in this context. We believe that it is 2.2 percent with a probability of 0.9, but there is a 0.1 probability that the true trend is actually only 0.1 percent per year. Moreover, macroeconomic catastrophes will strike with a probability of 1.7 percent every year. In this case, the growth rate for the year is normally distributed with a dismal mean of −30 percent and a standard deviation of 25 percent.

These beliefs combine catastrophic events à la Barro with some deep uncertainty about the true trend of the economy. Assuming this could be a reasonable representation of our collective aspirations and beliefs, we can use the following investment decision rules. These rules are based on my computation of the term structures of the risk-free discount rates and the macroeconomic risk premium under these assumptions. These term structures are illustrated in figure 4.1.

For safe projects or projects with idiosyncratic risks, a risk-free discount rate of around 1.5 percent should be used to value socioeconomic benefits materializing within the next few decades. For safe projects with long-lasting impacts, no discounting at all should be used.

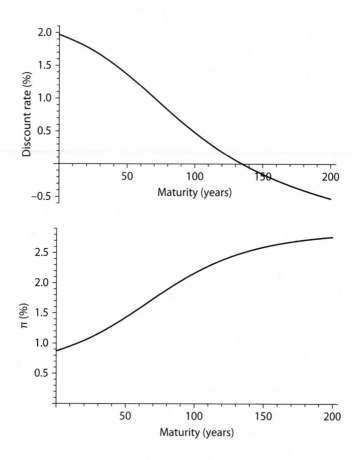

Figure 4.1 The term structures of the risk-free discount rates r and the macro-economic risk premium π under the assumptions made in this section.

When a project has a non-zero beta, a risk premium should
be added to the risk-free discount rate just described. This
risk premium equals the project's beta multiplied by the
macroeconomic risk premium. For maturities between
zero and fifty years, a macroeconomic risk premium of

around 1 percent should be used. For maturities measured
in centuries, the macroeconomic risk premium is around
2.5 percent.

Of course, these recommendations are very sensitive to
both the agreed-upon degree of collective inequality aversion and the agreed-upon probabilistic beliefs about the evolution of prosperity in the decades and centuries to come.

Observe that the risk-adjusted discount rate can increase
with maturity if the beta of the project is large enough.
This is because the term structure of the risk premium
is increasing, and its slope is proportional to the beta of
the project. In Gollier (2008), I showed that, under some
conditions, the critical beta for which the term structure
of the risk-adjusted discount rate starts increasing with
maturity is equal to half the degree of inequality aversion.
Under our assumption, this is $\beta = 1$.

These recommendations typically yield discount rates
lower than market rates of return. In this sense, they provide a measure of financial markets' short-termism. If these
recommendations are implemented, we will do more for the
future than what markets actually do today. However, the
long-term macroeconomic risk premium of 3 percent is not
far from the deleveraged equity premium observed on financial markets. This implies that the current price signal of risk
efficiently assists investors and entrepreneurs in their decision to favor risky projects over safer ones.

These recommended discount rates express our ethical
values toward risk and time. Note that the model I present in
this book to support these normative recommendations is

equivalent in nature to the consumption capital asset pricing model (CCAPM) formula first developed by Lucas (1978). But my approach differs from this CCAPM theory in many dimensions. My aim here is to evaluate actions with very distant costs and benefits. The socioeconomic impacts contain purely financial benefits together with extra-financial performances, such as those that are social and environmental. Contrary to Lucas (1978), I am not directly interested in explaining observed prices on financial markets. My approach is normative, and the utilitarian welfare function I use here has an ethical dimension, in particular in terms of collective inequality aversion. In short, my aim is not to try to explain what financial prices are, but what they should be.

A CRITIQUE OF EXISTING PROCEDURES TO EVALUATE PUBLIC POLICIES

Hopefully, not all decisions are left to the markets. Because of the presence of externalities and public goods, efficient governments have a crucial role to play in fixing the price of these externalities, many of them associated with pollution and sustainable development. They must also provide many basic types of infrastructure that serve as public goods, such as schools, transportation networks, and hospitals. The benefits of such goods are very persistent, and so public economists have focused on the question of what discount rate should be used to evaluate and prioritize them. This has led to different approaches by different countries.

Under the Nixon administration, the Office of Management and Budget attempted to standardize discounting methods across federal agencies and required the use of a 10 percent rate (OMB 1972). In 1992, the rate was revised down to 7 percent on the basis that "7 percent is the estimated return of private capital in the economy" (OMB 2003). In 2003, the Office of Management and Budget revised this rate downward again to 3 percent, while requesting a sensitivity analysis by using the former rate of 7 percent. This 3 percent rate was justified at the time because it represented "the real rate of return on long government bonds." The 3 percent rate actually corresponds to the average real yield of ten-year Treasury bonds in the United States between 1973 and 2003. The guideline recommends using the 7 percent discount rate when a public investment is financed through a substitution from the productive capital of the economy, whereas the 3 percent rate should be used if a public investment is financed through a reduction of aggregate consumption. This is of course total nonsense. In reality, how a project is financed is not what matters. The crucial difference between the two discount rates is the equity premium, so the differentiating factor is whether the project has a risk profile closer to that of a portfolio of diversified equity or that of a U.S. Treasury bond. Arrow et al. (2013, 2014) recommend a lower discount rate in the United States to evaluate projects whose impacts are more distant in the future.

In the United Kingdom, the Treasury (HM Treasury 2003) built a set of rules to evaluate public policies by publishing a "Green Book." This guide recommends a 3.5 percent rate, with a reduced rate of 1 percent for flows occurring beyond two hundred years.

In France, France Stratégie (previously the Commissariat Général au Plan) traditionally determines the discount rate to suit the macroeconomic and industrial plans in place. This rate was 7 percent in the Fifth Plan (1966–1970), 10 percent in the Sixth Plan (1971–1975), and 9 percent in the Seventh and Eighth Plans (1976–1985). Between 1985 and 2005, an 8 percent rate prevailed, based on the argument of the return of private capital, similar to the United States in the 1960s (CGP 1985). In 1985, a drastic reduction to 4 percent was introduced, with a reduction to only 2 percent for flows occurring beyond thirty years (Lebègue 2005) and an indication that a project-specific risk premium must be added to the risk-free discount rate. In 2011, Gollier (2011) quantified this risk premium. Finally, Quinet (2013) revised all these rates, with a risk-free discount rate ranging from 2.5 percent (short term) to 1.5 percent (long term) and a macroeconomic risk premium ranging from 1.5 percent (short term) to 3 percent (long term).

According to whether the country is eligible or noneligible for the European Cohesion Fund, the European Commission (2008) recommends using a real discount rate of 3.5 percent or 5.5 percent, respectively.

Except recently for France, a striking common feature among these rules is the absence of any attempt to disentangle the two components of the discount rate: the price of time and the price of risk. In the United States, for example, the two discount rates of 3 percent and 7 percent clearly demonstrate a hesitation between the risk-free rate (the return on Treasury bonds) and the risk-adjusted rate (the return of stocks). Using a single discount rate independent of the risk profile of the public investment project under scrutiny is inefficient. If the selected discount rate is an average of the risk-free and risk adjusted rates, then too many risky projects and too few safe projects will be implemented. Moreover, this is dangerous, because it will provide a (bad) incentive in public–private partnerships for the private sector to transfer the risk of projects to the public sector.

More positive is the clear trend to reduce the public discount rate over the last two decades. This is partly a result of the parallel reduction of interest rates in the Western world during this period. But it's also in line with the recommendations justified here. The decision to use lower discount rates for longer maturities, as has been implemented in the United Kingdom since 2003, may be problematic if the discount rate is not differentiated on the basis of the risk profile of the project. Indeed, as I said earlier, the risk-adjusted discount rate should decrease with maturities only if the beta of the project is smaller than unity.

THE SOCIOECONOMIC BETA

A possible reason for why the public sector resists basing the discount rate on the project-specific risk profile is because the risk profile may be difficult to measure. Although it can be summarized by a single number (the beta of the project), its estimation may require sophisticated data collection and analysis and the use of high-level financial tools and concepts.

Remember that the beta of a project is the income elasticity of its future socioeconomic benefits; that is, the percent by which the benefit increases in expectation when the GDP per capita increases by 1 percent. For example, if the expected benefit increases by 5 percent under these circumstances, the beta of the project is 5, and future expected benefits should be discounted by a rate equaling the risk-free rate plus five times the macroeconomic risk premium. The estimation of the income elasticity of a project can be obtained by using data about benefits generated by similar projects to econometrically analyze their statistical relation with aggregate income.

A good example is any project whose main benefit is to save lives or reduce mortality risk in the future. In chapter 2, I defined the notion of the value of statistical life, which is the monetary equivalent of the benefit associated with reducing mortality risk. In an international context comparing the United States and Bangladesh, I discussed the income elasticity of the value of statistical life, concluding from a survey of the literature (Hammitt and Robinson 2011) that it should be around 1. In an intergenerational context, this suggests that projects whose main goal is to reduce mortality risk in the future should have a unit beta. Their risk-adjusted discount rate should be the sum of the risk-free rate and the macroeconomic risk premium. Its term structure should be flat.

But often, we don't have the data to estimate income elasticities, either because the project has never been tested before or because these data have never been collected. An economic model is then necessary. Let's consider a very specific example to illustrate this.

Frédéric Cherbonnier and I recently worked with the electricity industry to estimate the beta of investment projects aimed at reinforcing the transnational electricity transportation network, as the renewable electricity revolution in Europe necessitates rethinking the electric grid. One of the questions we tried to answer was, from the point of view of France, what is the socioeconomic benefit of increasing the capacity of a high-voltage line with Germany?

The value of such an expansion is mainly the ability to transfer electricity from a country where it is less costly to produce to one where it is more costly to produce. For example, France exports its cheap, surplus nuclear electricity to Germany when Germany is lacking wind and sun and must rely on its costly coal technology to produce electricity. Thus, such an expansion would reduce both total cost and environmental damage. For France, the benefit of the line equals the difference between the marginal cost of electricity between Germany and France (when it's positive), which includes the social cost of carbon associated with the mitigation of carbon dioxide emissions that this export would generate.

One can estimate a stochastic model linking the demand and supply of electricity in the two countries with various risk factors, such as differential weather conditions, the availability of various production units, and economic growth in the two countries. What is the income elasticity of this benefit for France? In this model, with a fixed production structure, an increase in income in France increases the demand for electricity in that country and reduces the excess nuclear energy available for sale to Germany. Thus, the French income elasticity of the benefit of a marginal increase in the capacity of the Franco-German line is negative, as its socioeconomic benefit drops when income increases. This implies that the investment project should be evaluated by using a discount rate lower than the risk-free interest rate. It is the consequence of the insurance benefit of the project; that is, it hedges the macroeconomic risk.

As this example shows, estimating socioeconomic betas is a complex matter, and as a result, most evaluators prefer short cuts—such as using sectoral betas. As discussed by Krüger, Landier, and Thesmar (2015), an economic sector is made up of a portfolio of investments that are sometimes very different in nature, involving risks with heterogeneous betas. The sectoral beta is simply a weighted average of the betas of investments in the sector. Using the same sectoral beta to evaluate different projects within a sector would amount to taking advantage of the presence of low-beta projects in the sector so as to reduce the sector's cost of capital and finance high-beta projects at a low cost. Doing so would lead to an inefficient allocation of capital in the economy. Likewise, during a year like 2016, when there was a low rate of return on sovereign bonds in Europe and the United States, people took advantage of the low cost of public capital to invest in large public infrastructure projects. Admittedly, this low level of short-term interest linked to poor growth prospects is a valid argument for investing in low-risk, short-term projects. But the macroeconomic risk premium remains high, which should push these countries to maintain a higher discount rate for projects characterized by positive betas.

THE CLIMATE BETA AND THE
SOCIAL COST OF CARBON

Over the last two decades, economic interest in long-term discounting mostly came from the debate on climate change and the measurement of the social cost of carbon. The social cost of carbon is the risk-adjusted discounted value of the flow of expected damages generated by one ton more of carbon dioxide emitted in the atmosphere. Under the polluter-pays principle, it is socially desirable that every economic agent on this planet be exposed to a carbon price equal to the social cost of carbon to induce them to internalize the damages they impose on others by emitting carbon dioxide. This can be accomplished by imposing a tax on carbon dioxide emissions, with a tax per ton of carbon dioxide emitted equaling the social cost of carbon, or alternatively by organizing a cap-and-trade system for emission permits and offering a total quantity of permits such that the equilibrium price of permits on the international market is equal to the social cost of carbon.

Because a large fraction of the damages from carbon release will materialize only in the distant future, the choice of the rate at which future climate damages should be discounted is a key variable in determining the social cost of carbon. The problem is that economists strongly disagree about what rate is appropriate. Martin Weitzman (2001) demonstrated this when, in 1998, he sent a simple questionnaire to more than 2,800 economists from the academic world asking the question: "Taking everything into consideration, at what real interest rate do you think we

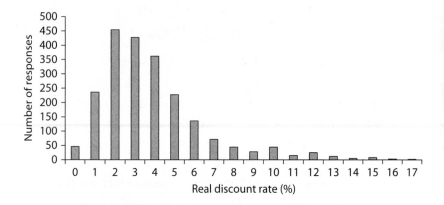

Figure 4.2   A histogram of individual estimates of the discount rate in a sample of 2,160 economists from academia.

Source: Weitzman 2001.

should update the benefits (expected) and costs (expected) of proposed projects that fight against climate change?" Weitzman got 2,160 replies, a frequency table for which is shown in figure 4.2. The mean is 3.96 percent, and the standard deviation is 2.94 percent. A striking feature of these results is the diversity of the individual estimations. This shows that, at least in 1998, there was no consensus on how to discount the future, and therefore no consensus on concepts such as short-termism and sustainable development. This lack of agreement was confirmed by a second study, which focused on fifty renowned economists, including Kenneth Arrow, Jean-Jacques Laffont, and Robert Merton. This expert group generated a similar diversity of replies, with a mean of 4.09 percent and a standard deviation of 3.07 percent.

Drupp et al. (2015) made a discounting survey of two hundred experts in the field. They focused on the discount rate to be used for risk-free benefits materializing in more than one hundred years. The mean long-term risk-free discount rate recommended by the respondents was 2.27 percent, with a range from 0 to 10 percent, and with more than 90 percent suggesting a long-term risk-free discount rate in the range of 1 to 3 percent was acceptable.

If future climate damages are certain, or are uncertain but uncorrelated with future consumption, one should use the long-term risk-free discount rate to assess them. Given my earlier analysis, this would mean no discounting at all, thus yielding a high social cost of carbon. Suppose alternatively that future climate damages are negatively correlated with future consumption. This means that climate damages are greatest when future consumption is lowest. In this context, fighting climate change would have the double advantage of reducing expected climate damages *and* hedging future macroeconomic risk. The insurance value of mitigation is expressed by a negative climate beta, yielding a discount rate lower than the long-term risk-free rate—in fact, this would imply a negative climate discount rate, and a very high social cost of carbon. If, on the contrary, climate damages are positively correlated with consumption, fighting climate change would raise the macroeconomic risk compared to the business-as-usual scenario. This means a positive climate beta, a relatively high climate discount rate, and a relatively low social cost of carbon.

Existing estimations of the social cost of carbon range from around $10 to $150 per ton of carbon dioxide emitted.

Nordhaus (2008), who typically uses a discount rate of 5 percent, obtained estimations of the social cost of carbon at the lower end of this range, whereas Stern (2007), who implicitly uses a discount rate of around 1 percent, obtained estimations at the upper end of the range. This implies that Nordhaus believes the climate beta is equal to or greater than 1—and thus that the climate discount rate should be roughly equal to the rate of return of a diversified portfolio of stocks—whereas Stern believes that the climate beta is zero and so the climate discount rate should be close to the risk-free rate in the economy. This disagreement is also expressed in comments that Weitzman (2001) received from some of the respondents to his discounting questionnaire:

> Another group of disgruntled participants wanted, in effect, to be supplied with the appropriate "beta" coefficient for the particular investment project in mind, since, according to them, it is impossible to speak meaningfully about a general discount rate "for projects to mitigate the effects of global climate change" without specifying more explicitly how the payoffs are supposed to be correlated with the performance of some index of alternative investments, like the value of the world's stock markets.

Determining the climate beta is thus crucial to solving the social cost of carbon controversy. What is the beta of an investment whose sole benefit would be a reduction of carbon dioxide emissions and thus an avoidance of climate damages in the future? As explained in Dietz, Gollier, and Kessler (2017), there are two competing hypotheses here.

If the main source of uncertainty for future generations comes from the risk surrounding exogenous economic growth, strong economic growth leads to high levels of carbon dioxide emissions. The consensus among climate modelers is that the climate damage function is increasing and convex. This means that the marginal damage increases with the concentration of greenhouse gases in the atmosphere. Therefore, high consumption growth rates go hand in hand with significant marginal climate damages. In this context, the climate beta is positive, and the climate discount rate is larger than the risk-free rate in order to recognize that fighting climate change does not bring any insurance benefit.

Suppose instead that the central source of long-term uncertainty comes from the unknown climate sensitivity to the concentration of greenhouse gases in the atmosphere. Climate sensitivity is defined as the increased average temperature of the atmosphere when one doubles the concentration of greenhouse gases in the atmosphere. Despite intensive research on climate sensitivity over the last twenty years, this parameter is still highly uncertain, mostly owing to the potential for vicious cycles in climate dynamics. For example, some experts believe that the increased temperature will induce permafrost to melt, implying a huge additional release of greenhouse gases in the atmosphere. Other suggested consequences include a reduction in the albedo of ice and snow caps and a dampening effect of increased cloud coverage or of photosynthesis. If we believe that climate sensitivity is a main source of risk for future generations, then we get a negative-beta story. Indeed, strong climate sensitivity leads simultaneously to significant damages, low consumption, and a significant benefit of emission reduction efforts today, and thus a negative climate beta.

The winner of these two competing stories depends upon what source of long-term risk is considered most important. The uncertainty about climate sensitivity is large, but it is in fact much smaller than the uncertainty affecting growth in the long run. Stern (2007), for example, shows that a low climate sensitivity will reduce consumption in two hundred years by 5 percent, whereas a high climate sensitivity will reduce it by 35 percent, a discrepancy in consumption of 30 percent. Suppose alternatively that we're not sure about whether the consumption growth rate will be 0 percent or 2 percent per year in the future. The discrepancy in consumption here is 5,400 percent. This is why Dietz, Gollier, and Kessler (2017) obtained a net effect largely favorable to the positive-beta story, with a climate beta of around 1. This is in line with the recent results of Nordhaus (2011), which summarize the outcome of Monte-Carlo simulations of the much more sophisticated RICE-2011 model with sixteen sources of uncertainty: "Those states in which the global temperature increase is particularly high are also ones in which we are on average richer in the future." Thus, the fight against climate change does not seem to have a benefit in terms of reducing the global risk borne by future generations.

The positive and relatively large climate beta brings bad news and good news for proponents of an immediate and aggressive fight against climate change. The bad news is that the climate discount rate is large, with a negative impact on the price one should put on carbon. The good news is as follows. Remember that the beta of an action is the income elasticity of its benefit. A large beta means that the benefit will increase faster with time, in parallel with economic growth. Therefore, increasing the beta increases both the numerator (the future expected benefit) and the denominator (the discount rate) in the present valuation formula. It happens that the first effect vastly dominates the second effect, so that a large climate beta is associated with a high social cost of carbon.

VALUING NATURAL CAPITAL

An even more complex valuation problem concerns natural assets and their preservation. Our attitude toward natural capital—such as water, biodiversity, fossil energy reserves, and unspoiled natural sites—is determined by the way we price it. But most natural assets generate ecological services that will persist for centuries, and deep uncertainties surround the valuation of these services by future generations. This implies that there is no consensus about how to price natural capital. For this reason, the notion of pricing natural capital remained until now a metaphor rather than an instrument (Fenichel and Abbott 2014).

As explained in chapter 3 when I discussed the notion of ecological discounting, the monetary value of the services generated by natural assets will fluctuate through time in relation to their increased relative scarcity. Most natural assets generate environmental services that differ from the consumption of manufactured goods and that have heterogeneous degrees of substitutability. For example, fossil fuel reserves could soon be easily substituted by renewable energies, but water reserves are much more difficult to substitute. Guesnerie (2004), Hoel and Sterner (2007), and Traeger (2011) have stressed the role of the evolution of relative prices in discounting. In a growing economy, the relative scarcity of the nonsubstitutable services of natural capital that cannot be expanded will increase, thereby increasing their relative value for future generations.

Consider a natural asset whose services are highly non-substitutable and cannot be expanded by human actions. The combination of these two characteristics implies that the socioeconomic value of this asset will have a high income elasticity, and a high beta. Because of the positive beta, future expected benefits will be discounted at a higher rate—bad news for proponents of aggressive preservation policies—but in a growing economy, future expected benefits will be larger. The bottom line is a positive effect: Less substitutable assets should be more highly valued.

The substitutability of scarce environmental goods by manufactured goods is central to any cost–benefit analysis of environmental policies and to the notion of sustainability. In the late seventeenth century, the French administration expanded oak forests to ensure they would have the material needed to build ships two centuries later to fight British naval forces—long before realizing that oak would be substituted by steel. More recently, we've seen wars fought for the control of oil fields—but in the near future we'll likely realize that oil can well be substituted by nonconventional gas reserves and renewable sources of energy. Optimistic futurists believe that the need for material goods and disappearing natural capital will be reduced or even eliminated by new technologies. These stories tell us that the future degree of substitutability of most natural assets is highly uncertain. So is their beta. Gollier (2015) explores the consequences of this uncertainty on asset valuation.

THE PRECAUTIONARY PRINCIPLE AND THE OPTION VALUE TO DELAY IRREVERSIBLE ACTIONS

Deep uncertainty is highly associated with learning. For example, we will probably soon learn whether technological progress can make photovoltaic panels a viable alternative to fossil fuels on a large scale. Among other things, this would require progress on battery efficiency and other forms of electricity storage. If this is attainable, then climate change may not be a problem after all. Alternatively, we may learn within a decade or two that climate sensitivity is much higher than expected. We could also learn that we have crossed the tipping point of greenhouse gas concentrations in the atmosphere, with the melting permafrost releasing vast quantities of greenhouse gases that will warm us for centuries. What we don't know today but will know in the future has important consequences for the way we should manage risk. Economists and finance researchers have developed a theory of real option in which the cost–benefit analysis technique is enriched to include the option value to postpone decisions involving irreversible consequences (see, for example, Dixit and Pindyck 1994).

If one makes an irreversible decision before accessing information that helps measure the creation of socioeconomic value for the decision, one loses the possibility of acting more efficiently. For example, building a new coal-fired power plant today that will emit carbon dioxide during the next three or four decades is dangerous and irresponsible in the current context, as we are not sure what social cost of carbon this plant will face during that period. We know that implementing a social cost of carbon of around $30 per ton of carbon dioxide emitted will make that plant noncompetitive compared to a combined-cycle gas power plant. Moreover, one will continue to learn about technological progress in the photovoltaic and windmill industries, which are two significant sources of uncertainty for the coal industry. In this context, the option to wait for more information is valuable, but it is also costly because of the missed opportunities of social value creation in the short run. The option value to wait is the monetary value of the information; that is, the sure increase in consumption that has the same effect on the utilitarian social welfare as obtaining the necessary information. The optimal timing of the decision is a best compromise between the cost of the delay and its information benefit.

Using real option valuation in cost–benefit analysis is not an easy matter, as it means quantifying both the current uncertainty and the learning process that will resolve the uncertainty. It also means identifying the sources of irreversibility in the system under scrutiny. Let's re-examine the fight against climate change from this point of view.

The sources of uncertainty and learning with regard to climate change abound, with some likely to be resolved faster than others. Scientific uncertainties on tipping points and vicious reactions in the climate system will be more clearly understood within the next few years or so. At the same time, nobody yet knows whether carbon sequestration (or other geoengineering techniques) will be technically and economically feasible in the future—a crucial question for fossil fuel–rich countries in the decades to come. And nobody can credibly tell us whether the energy efficiency of photovoltaic cells will continue to improve in the future at the same speed as they have done over the last four decades. How should we determine the optimal timing of installing capital-intensive renewable energy capacity (e.g., photovoltaic panels, windmills) on a massive scale in this context?

Two sources of irreversibility should be of primary concern. First, investing in renewable energy capacity is capital irreversible, in the sense that photovoltaic panels and windmills cannot be used for anything else if these technologies become obsolete in the future, either because of creative destruction or because the price of carbon is too low to make renewable energy economically viable. In this scenario, the renewable energy capacity will be a stranded asset. Capital irreversibility is an argument for delaying the implementation of green technologies. Second, the alternative to renewable energy capacity is to burn fossil fuels. In the absence of a viable sequestration technology, emitting carbon dioxide into the atmosphere is irreversible. This ecological irreversibility is catastrophic if we learn in the future that we have passed the tipping point of greenhouse gas concentrations in the atmosphere. Observe that here, it is inaction—rather than action—that yields irreversible impacts. This ecological irreversibility tends to favor an early investment in building renewable capacity. The jury is still out on the net effect of these two opposing, but real, options. However, discussions about the optimal timing of implementing green technologies should not prevent our first-order analysis of the valuation of the long-term benefits of these technologies.

Preventive actions are also natural candidates for the application of real option theory. For many environmental and health risks, the probability distribution of future damages is unknown, and more information about them will be obtained in the future. In addition to the climate change problem, we can think of the risk of cancer following exposure to asbestos in the 1960s and 1970s, when the risk was still not completely understood. Uncertainty about tobacco risk, about transfused blood at the outbreak of the HIV crisis, or about certain vaccines with side effects are other examples from the past in which the value of waiting for better information was used to postpone public intervention. But such waits have led to notorious scandals. In reaction, new decision principles have been imposed. The precautionary principle is the best example of this. Its wording in Principle 15 of the 1992 Rio Declaration on Environment and Development states that "where there are threats of serious or irreversible damage, lack of full scientific certainty shall not be used as a reason for postponing cost-effective measures to prevent environmental degradation." The precautionary principle takes a committed stand against "learn-then-act" or "wait-and-see" strategies in favor of early preventive actions (Gollier and Treich 2003). One can trace the origin of the precautionary principle to 1984, at the First International

Conference on the Protection of the North Sea. It has since flourished in international statements of policy, such as the Maastricht Treaty and the Rio Declaration. These days, the precautionary principle is mostly used in European legislations. Under this principle, in the United Kingdom, the country worst affected by the crisis of mad cow disease in the early 1990s (with more than 180,000 cattle infected), the decision was made to slaughter 4.4 million cows during the eradication program.

The precautionary principle is a new moral principle. It is not clear whether it is linked to utilitarianism, because it does not provide much detail about how to make it operational. Most interpretations of the precautionary principle are in fact incompatible with the moral principles upon which the arguments in this book are based. For example, one extreme interpretation is in favor of an "enlightened catastrophism," in which our actions under uncertainty should be made under an assumption that "the worst is certain." This is related to a theory of ambiguity aversion. Empirical studies tend to show that people prefer to earn 100 with a probability of $1/2$ than to earn 100 with an unknown probability whose mean is $1/2$ (Ellsberg 1961). In the maxmin version of this theory (Gilboa and Schmeidler 1989), when people face some ambiguity about the true probability of an event, they select the action that maximizes the lowest expected utility among the different plausible probabilities. This is a strong form of pessimism, which may explain the behavior of real people facing deep uncertainties. This form of ambiguity aversion is related to Rawlsian prioritarianism, in which all the weight is put on the utility of the poorest person in the welfare function. This is what an ambiguity-averse person would do under the veil of ignorance when they are also ignorant of the wealth distribution in the society. But one should recognize that earning 100 with an unknown probability that has an equal probability of taking a value of either 1/3 or 2/3 is equivalent to earning 100 with a probability of 1/2. Because the utilitarian social welfare measured by discounted expected utility is linear in probabilities, one should be neutral to any mean-preserving spread in probabilities.

Refusing to compound probabilities based on scientific knowledge is a form of obscurantism. Because there is no limit on the definition of the worst scenario, catastrophism does not provide an operational rule to judge the social optimality of an action ex ante. And if it did, it would lead us to annihilate scientific and technological innovations. Less extreme forms of ambiguity aversion (see, for example, Klibanoff, Marinacci, and Mukerji 2005) are useful in explaining how people behave in the face of uncertainty. But ambiguity aversion has no strong normative appeal, and it has no obvious translation into operational rules for public action.

As explained by Fischhoff (2007), for example, many people are victims of hindsight bias, or the "knew-it-all-along" effect. This is the natural inclination to evaluate an action ex post as if the outcome were highly predictable, using information that was not available at the time of the decision. Such a bias makes the life of the decision-maker quite dangerous. In the face of deep uncertainty and learning about the benefit of some preventive effort, decision-makers may make two "probabilistic errors."

First, they may believe that the risk is real and catastrophic. This would induce them to implement costly preventive actions. If one learns ex post that the risk was small, the situation can be a source of embarrassment. It has been suggested that the 2009 swine flu (H1N1) outbreak—an influenza pandemic—is an example of this, as many countries spent billions of dollars on vaccines before realizing that the pandemic was much weaker than initially anticipated. It has also been suggested that the mad cow disease outbreak was another illustration of this type of situation, but a counterfactual analysis is not easy to perform.

The second type of "error" may emerge when decision-makers initially believe that the risk is negligible, thereby inducing them to do nothing. If one learns ex post that the risk is catastrophic, this can also be embarrassing. Typical examples include decisions made in response to the dangers of asbestos and tobacco exposure worldwide and to the HIV-infected blood transfusion scandal in France.

It is a matter of fact that the vox populi judges the second type of error much more harshly than the first. This leads prudent politicians to hedge the risk of the second type of error by favoring strong early preventive actions, invoking the precautionary principle as an excuse.

An alternative, simpler, interpretation of the precautionary principle is that the public sector in Europe underestimates the value of life and the value of environmental assets. Because most of the benefits of public prevention efforts concern mortality and environmental risks, the precautionary principle expresses a collective willingness to rebalance cost–benefit analysis in favor of health and environmental protection. Whatever the truth is, my recommendation is to perform cost–benefit analysis under uncertainty by correctly measuring cost and the option value to wait, using the best available information, and by updating this information whenever it emerges.

SUMMARY

Risk aversion is a ubiquitous characteristic of human beings. It makes us eager to share risk with others, to insure against large risks, and to invest in prevention. It makes us reluctant to take risks that cannot be washed out by mutualization and diversification. But most actions made in the name of a better future affect the collective risk borne by future generations. Evaluating these actions by the discounted value of their expected net benefits fails to recognize the importance of risk aversion in the measurement of intergenerational welfare.

One should give a bonus in cost–benefit analysis to any action that hedges collective risk, and one should penalize any action that increases it. But many, if not most, investments for the future tend to increase collective risk, as their benefits are larger when consumption is greater. In consequence, penalizing risk-increasing actions reduces investment as a whole, which inhibits economic growth. One is thus confronted with a risk–return tradeoff, where "return" should here be understood as the collective benefit of economic growth. Has the compromise between these two contradicting objectives been overly favorable to the maximization of the expected social return, or to the minimization of risk? Put simply, is the world too risky?

In full coherence with the moral principles discussed earlier, I have shown that it is socially desirable to adjust the discount rate to the risk profile of each investment project by adding a risk premium. This project-specific risk premium is the product of the normative beta of the project by the macroeconomic risk premium. This beta is the percentage increase in the socioeconomic value—including financial, social, and environmental benefits—of the project when aggregate consumption increases by 1 percent. It measures the contribution of the project to collective risk. The macroeconomic risk premium is the key variable controlling the intensity of risk undertaken in the economy. I have shown that the same ingredients that justify a decreasing term structure for the risk-free discount rate also justify an increasing term structure for the risk premium. Deep uncertainties, in particular, magnify the long-term macroeconomic risk. Assuming a degree of inequality aversion of 2, I have concluded here that it is reasonable to impose a macroeconomic risk premium of 2.5 percent for investment projects with long-lasting financial, social, and environmental impacts.

In our decentralized economies, investment decisions are mostly made on financial markets. Markets penalize firms that increase the aggregate risk (collected in investors' diversified portfolios) by raising their cost of capital. The 1-to-2.5 percent risk premium invoked earlier is very much in line with the equity premium imposed by markets on riskier firms, given the fact that the beta of diversified equity is around 3. So, it is reasonable to conclude that the price signal sent to market participants about how much risk they should undertake is in line with intergenerational welfare. Much more worrying is the absence of any formal penalization of risk in the evaluation of public policies and public investments in most countries. In summary, the private sector has the right incentives to internalize the social cost of the risks it undertakes, but the public sector is incentivized to take too much risk. In particular, the public sector does not recognize the social benefit of public projects that hedge macroeconomic risk.

CONCLUSION

opulism is on the rise everywhere, and the fairness of
public decisions is being questioned by a growing number of people on both sides of the Atlantic. For these citizens,
the elites are not only believed to be corrupt, they are also
criticized for not sharing the values of the people they represent and for making decisions that are incompatible with
the national common good. For example, Donald Trump
claimed during the 2016 presidential campaign that the
Environmental Protection Agency was pushing too much in
favor of the environment and not enough in favor of protect-
ing American jobs.

At the same time, financial markets and their leaders
are subject to intense critiques about the priorities and values they impose on citizens and the democratic order. The
"Occupy Wall Street" movement and its multiple offshoots
around the world have focused their resentment on banks
as representative of the old financial order, which should be
overthrown. Many voters in the French presidential election
of May 2017 refused to decide between two "evils," a fascist

and a banker, referring to the two finalists of the runoff. For modern populists and anticapitalist activists, the financial capitalism that ruled the world over the last century is the common enemy. Financial capitalism imposes its diktat by imposing financial constraints on economic agents that are often perceived as unfair or inefficient. When these constraints are imposed on governments, such as in Greece since 2011, financial institutions appear to be imposing priorities and values that are superior to those emanating from democratic institutions.

This political, financial, and economic turmoil calls for an analysis of whether financial markets can—or cannot—decentralize an efficient allocation of the scarce resources in our economy. There are strong arguments for believing that financial markets are not good at eliciting our collective values or providing the right price signals for individuals and companies to align private interests with the public good. Agency problems such as moral hazard and adverse selection inhibit market efficiency, whereas the inability to trade with future generations make markets unable to efficiently value assets and investments that benefit future generations. More importantly, corporate profits do not internalize the full set of impacts from the production process on social welfare. For example, the emission of greenhouse gases remains mostly free of charge around the world, in spite of the destructive impact such emissions have on people's welfare. Don't ask financial liberalism to fix this problem in a deregulated world.

If markets are unable to aggregate our collective values, what principles should govern the evaluation of our private and public acts? How should we, for example, compare environmental protection against job protection, lives in Bangladesh versus purchasing power in Europe, workplace safety against corporate profits, reduced inequality versus growth, or more consumption today against more consumption in two hundred years? The populist turmoil also requires us to elaborate morally acceptable principles to determine the way society should value these actions. Confronted with incredulous and disappointed citizens, experts and politicians should make their recommendations and decisions more transparently linked to fundamental social, environmental, and ethical values. Debating these values should be at the root of our democracy, potentially with different political parties defending different values. Elections should allow citizens to vote on these values, and elected politicians should use the values supported by a majority of voters to evaluate the alternative political options they face during their mandates.

The public sector has its own sources of inefficiency, in the absence of any obvious allocation mechanism such as the market institution. It has therefore been confronted with these valuation problems since Western governments began attempting to evaluate their own public policies after the Second World War. The question of the efficiency of each dollar of public spending is particularly crucial in states where its share in GDP is large, such as in France (57 percent) or Finland (58 percent), the two leaders in this domain among OECD countries. Many countries have established a set of implicit prices that public institutions must use when performing an evaluation of their actions. Today, most policies in Western Europe and North America are evaluated by using a price for human lives, time lost, natural assets, carbon dioxide, and so on, in sectors as diverse as energy, transportation, health, science, and education. These prices are subject to much debate among experts. These debates remain inaccessible to the public, and this is unacceptable. Many citizens, businesspeople, and investors are also eager to contribute to the resolution of the great challenges of our time. Some households are willing to give up some of the return from their savings if it will be allocated in socially responsible investments funds, but most of these funds have not been able to create transparent rules to evaluate their actions. Many companies are also interested in behaving in a more socially responsible way. But here, too, there is no consensus about how corporate social responsibility should interfere with the fiduciary duty of a firm with respect to its shareholders to determine decision rules.

Most of this book has been devoted to the discussion of two prices that drive most financial decisions: the price of time, which is the interest rate, and the price of risk. The choice of interest rate drives the collective degree of our long-termism. It determines whether one does enough for the future. Too high an interest rate inhibits economic agents to invest for the future. On the contrary, if the interest rate is too low, entrepreneurs will be induced to invest too much, forcing people to sacrifice too much of their current well-being to finance these projects. So what is the right interest rate? I have shown that there are two driving forces in the determination of a socially desirable interest rate. The first force is based on the assumption that we are collectively averse to inequality. In a growing economy, investing for the future raises intergenerational inequality. From this viewpoint, the interest rate should be interpreted as the minimal rate of return on a safe investment that compensates for the increased intergenerational inequality that the investment generates. After all, if consumption per capita continues to grow at 2 percent per year as it did in the past, people living two centuries from now will consume fifty times more quality-weighted goods and services than we do now. The second force originates from the fact that we collectively face huge uncertainties about the true prosperity of humankind on this planet. This should induce us to maintain an interest rate low enough to induce more long-termism than if such uncertainty did not exist. In this book, I have attempted to calibrate the different parameters that describe both our collective ethical attitude toward inequalities and our beliefs about our collective destiny. This challenging exercise has led me to support a risk-free discount rate slightly below twice the anticipated growth rate of consumption for benefits materializing within the next two to three decades. But for longer maturities, the deep uncertainties surrounding the destiny of humanity should induce us to use a discount rate close to 0 percent for safe projects; that is, no discounting.

The price of risk is the other crucial price signal used by economic agents to determine their investment decisions. The main driver here is the corporate cost of capital, which is increasing in the contribution of the portfolio of a corporation's investments to the macroeconomic risk. If this risk premium is too small, economic agents are incentivized to invest in very risky projects in a casino capitalism, but this may be beneficial for economic growth and employment in expectation. If this risk premium is too large, economic agents will be discouraged from taking risk, thereby hindering innovation and growth. The choice of the socially desirable risk premium depends upon our collective degree of risk aversion. But under the Rawlsian principle of the veil of ignorance, risk aversion and inequality aversion are the same concept. In coherence with the calibration of the interest rate, I have concluded that a risk premium of around 1 percent should be used at short maturities for projects with a risk profile similar to the risk on aggregate consumption. This is in line with the short-dated asset prices observed on financial markets over the last century. But because of the deep uncertainties surrounding the distant future, a larger risk premium of around 2.5 percent should be used for very long maturities.

These conclusions support an intelligent use of the standard tool of cost–benefit analysis in which the system of values used to perform the evaluation is based on valuation principles in line with a transparent description of our social aspirations. Because of the many sources of failure in financial capitalism, these socially desirable values may be far from the corresponding prices observed on markets. In this book, I have described a set of moral principles that I believe most economists would accept as a normative basis for policy evaluation. Combining these principles with a reasonable description about our collective destiny, I have derived my conclusions concerning the way one should penalize actions that ask for immediate sacrifices or that increase risk. The quality of these conclusions is not better than the premises upon which they are based. It is up to society as a whole to decide which moral principles should form the cornerstone of collective decision-making and which beliefs about our collective destiny are acceptable. My legitimacy as an economist is extremely weak for this purpose. However, I hope that this book will spark a collective debate about these questions: questions I consider crucial for the future of our democracies.

TECHNICAL APPENDIX

In this appendix, I derive the rules to price assets in the benchmark case used in the finance literature. It is assumed that consumption per capita follows a geometric Brownian motion with a known mean μ and a known volatility σ. I normalize current consumption to 1. These assumptions mean that the logarithm of consumption at any future date t is normally distributed with mean μt and variance $\sigma^2 t$. It is also assumed that the index of relative risk aversion γ is constant so marginal utility $U'(c_t)$ at date t is $c_t^{-\gamma}$.

Consider first a safe investment that generates a sure net benefit b in t years per dollar invested today. Because the implementation of the project affects consumption only today and at date t, we can measure the impact of investing k dollars in this project by the following function:

$$V(k) = U(c_0 - k) + EU(c_t + kb). \tag{1}$$

This is the unweighted sum of the expected utility of the two generations affected by the project. A small investment in this project increases intergenerational social welfare if, and only if, $V'(0)$ is positive. This condition is equivalent to requiring that the net present value $-1 + b\exp(-r^f t)$ of the project be positive, with a discount rate r being defined as follows:

$$r^f = -\frac{1}{t}\log\left(\frac{EU'(c_t)}{U'(c_0)}\right) = -\log\left(Ec_t^{-\gamma}\right). \qquad (2)$$

Here, we need to compute the expectation of the power of a log-normally distributed variable. This is good news, because we can use the following standard result of the classical asset pricing literature (see, for example, Gollier 2012):

Lemma: If $\log(x)$ is normally distributed with mean m and variance s^2, then Ex^k is equal to $\exp(km + 0.5k^2s^2)$.

This result is implicit in the groundbreaking works of Merton (1969) and Samuelson (1969), for example. Using this Lemma in equation (2) directly implies that the socially desirable risk-free discount rate equals

$$r^f = \gamma\mu - 0.5\gamma^2\sigma^2. \qquad (3)$$

Compared to the Ramsey rule $r^f = \gamma\mu$, this result then tells us that the uncertainty affecting future consumption reduces the discount rate by $0.5\gamma^2\sigma^2$, which is a precautionary premium.

Let's now examine the case of a risky project generating a single benefit $b = c_t^\beta$ at date t for each dollar invested today. Parameter β is the elasticity of the net benefit with respect to aggregate consumption. It is also the socioeconomic (or CCAPM) beta of the project. The project increases V at the margin if

$$V'(0) = U'(c_0)\left[-1 + \frac{EbU'(c_t)}{U'(c_0)}\right] = U'(c_0)\left[-1 + e^{-rt}Eb\right]. \quad (4)$$

Thus, the project increases intergenerational welfare if the flow of expected net benefits discounted at the risk-adjusted rate r is positive. The risk-adjusted discount rate equals

$$r = -\frac{1}{t}\log\left(\frac{EbU'(c_t)}{EbU'(c_0)}\right) = -\frac{1}{t}\log\left(\frac{Ec_t^{\beta-\gamma}}{Ec_t^{\beta}}\right). \quad (5)$$

Using the Lemma twice to compute the two expectations appearing in the right-hand side of this equality yields

$$r = r^f + \beta\gamma\sigma^2. \quad (6)$$

In other words, the risk-adjusted discount rate used for this risk profile equals the risk-free rate r^f defined in equation (3), plus a risk premium equaling β times the systematic risk premium $\pi = \gamma\sigma^2$.

NOTES

1. COLLECTIVE ASPIRATIONS

1. A famous example is the "Monty Hall Problem," based on the American television game show *Let's Make a Deal* and named after its original host, Monty Hall. Suppose you're on a game show and are given a choice of three doors: Behind one door is a car; behind the other two, goats. You pick a door, say number 1, and the host, who knows what's behind the doors, opens another door, say number 3, which systematically has a goat behind it. The host then says to you, "Do you want to pick door number 2?" Most people would not switch their choice of door. However, not switching makes for a probability of winning of one in three, whereas switching increases the probability of winning to two out of three.

2. A function is concave if, and only if, its derivative is decreasing.

2. CHOICE AND MEASURE OF VALUES

1. To obtain this number, I have assumed that individual incomes are log-normally distributed; that is, that log income is normally distributed with mean μ and standard deviation σ. In this case, it can be shown that the impact

of income inequalities on social welfare is equivalent to a sure proportional reduction of income by $1 - \exp(-0.5\gamma\sigma^2)$. Acemoglu and Ventura (2002) documented a relatively stable standard deviation of log income in the world between 1960 and 1990, around $\sigma = 1$. Using $\gamma = 2$ implies that world income inequalities during that period yielded a reduction of worldwide social welfare equivalent to a sure proportional reduction of income by $1 - \exp(-1) = 63\%$.

3. DO WE DO ENOUGH FOR THE FUTURE?

1. This result comes from the fact that $\exp(-r)$ must be equal to $0.5 \exp(-0.04\gamma) + 0.5 \exp(-0\gamma)$. In the case of ambiguous probabilities, the maturity-specific discount rate rt must be such that $\exp(-r_t t)$ equals $0.5[0.9 \exp(-0.04\gamma t) + 0.1] + 0.5[0.1\exp(-0.04\gamma t) + 0.9]$.

BIBLIOGRAPHY

Acemoglu, D., and J. Ventura. 2002. "The World Income Distribution." *Quarterly Journal of Economics* 117: 658–94.

Andersson, M., P. Bolton, and F. Samama. 2015. "Hedging Climate Risk." *Financial Analysts Journal* 72(3): 13–32.

Arrow, K. J. 1963. "Liquidity Preference." Lecture VI in *Lecture Notes for Economics 285, The Economics of Uncertainty*, 33–53. Stanford, CT: Stanford University.

——. 1971. *Essays in the Theory of Risk Bearing*. Chicago: Markham.

——. 1999. "Discounting, Morality, and Gaming." In *Discounting and Intergenerational Equity*, edited by P. R. Portney and J. P. Weyant, 13–22. Washington, DC: Resources for the Future.

——. 2007. "Global Climate Change: A Challenge to Policy." *The Economists' Voice* 4(3): 1–5.

Arrow, K., M. Cropper, C. Gollier, B. Groom, G. Heal, R. Newell, W. Nordhaus, R. Pindyck, W. Pizer, P. Portney, T. Sterner, R. Tol, and M. Weitzman. 2013. "Determining Benefits and Costs for Future Generations." *Science* 341: 349–50.

——. 2014. "Should a Declining Discount Rate Be Used in Project Analysis?" *Review of Environmental Economics and Policy* 8: 145–63.

Arrow, K. J., and R. C. Lind. 1970. "Uncertainty and the Evaluation of Public Investment Decision." *American Economic Review* 60: 364–78.

BIBLIOGRAPHY

Atkinson, A. B. 1970. "On the Measurement of Inequality." *Journal of Economic Theory* 2: 244–63.

Atkinson, G., S. Dietz, J. Helgeson, C. Hepburn, and H. Sælen. 2009. "Siblings, Not Triplets: Social Preferences for Risk, Inequality and Time in Discounting Climate Change." *Economics: The Open Access, Open-Assessment E-Journal* 3 (2009-26): 1–30.

Bansal, R., and A. Yaron. 2004. "Risks for the Long Run: A Potential Resolution of Asset Pricing Puzzles." *Journal of Finance* 59: 1481–1509.

Barro, R. J. 2006. "Rare Disasters and Asset Markets in the Twentieth Century." *Quarterly Journal of Economics* 121: 823–66.

——. 2009. "Rare Disasters, Asset Prices, and Welfare Costs." *American Economic Review* 99: 243–64.

Barsky, R. B., F. T. Juster, M. S. Kimball, and M. D. Shapiro. 1997. "Preference Parameters and Behavioral Heterogeneity: An Experimental Approach in the Health and Retirement Study." *The Quarterly Journal of Economics* 112: 537–79.

Benabou, R., and J. Tirole. 2006. "Incentives and Prosocial Behavior." *American Economic Review* 96: 1652–78.

Bernoulli, D. 1954. "Exposition of a New Theory on the Measurement of Risk." *Econometrica* 22: 23–36.

Blanchard, O. J., and J. Tirole. 2008. "The Joint Design of Unemployment Insurance and Employment Protection: A First Pass." *The Journal of the European Economic Association* 6: 45–77.

Bonnefon, J.-F., A. Shariff, and I. Rahwan. 2016. "The Social Dilemma of Autonomous Vehicles." *Science* 352(6293): 1573–76.

Broome, J. 1991. *Weighing Goods: Equality, Uncertainty, and Time.* Oxford: Basil Blackwell.

Caiazzo, F., A. Ashok, I. A. Waitz, S. H. L. Yim, and S. R. H. Barrett. 2013. "Air Pollution and Early Deaths in the United States. Part I: Quantifying the Impact of Major Sectors in 2005." *Atmospheric Environment* 79: 198–208.

Clark, G. 2007. *A Farewell to Alms: A Brief Economic History of the World.* Princeton, NJ: Princeton University Press.

Cline, W. R. 1992. *The Economics of Global Warming*. Washington, DC: Peterson Institute for International Economics.

Collin-Dufresne, P., M. Johannes, and L. A. Lochstoer. 2016. "Parameter Learning in General Equilibrium: The Asset Pricing Implications." *American Economic Review* 106: 664–98.

Commissariat Général au Plan. 1985. *Recommandations sur les règles de calcul économique pour le 9e plan*. Letter to the Prime Minister, mimeo.

Cropper, M. L., J. K. Hammitt, and L. A. Robinson. 2011. "Valuing Mortality Risk Reductions: Progress and Challenges." *Annual Review of Resource Economics* 3: 313–36.

Dasgupta, P. 2008. "Comments on the Stern Review's Economics of Climate Change." *National Institute Economic Review* 199: 4–7.

Davis, L. W. 2004. "The Effect of Health Risk on Housing Values: Evidence from a Cancer Cluster." *American Economic Review* 94: 1693–1704.

Diamond, P. 1977. "A Framework for Social Security Analysis." *Journal of Public Economics* 8: 275–98.

Dietz, S., C. Gollier, and L. Kessler. 2017. "The Climate Beta." Journal of Environmental Economics and Management, forthcoming.

Dimson, E., P. Marsh, and M. Staunton. 2015. *Credit Suisse Global Investment Returns Sourcebook 2015*. Zurich: Credit Suisse Research Institute.

Dixit, A. K., and R. S. Pindyck. 1994. *Investment Under Uncertainty*. Princeton, NJ: Princeton University Press.

Drèze, J. H. 1981. "Inferring Risk Tolerance from Deductibles in Insurance Contracts." *Geneva Papers on Risk and Insurance* 6: 48–52.

Drèze, J. H., and C. Gollier. 1993. "Risk Sharing on the Labour Market and Second-Best Wage Rigidity." *European Economic Review* 37: 1457–82.

Drèze, J. H., and F. Modigliani. 1972. "Consumption Decisions Under Uncertainty." *Journal of Economic Theory* 5: 308–35.

Drupp, M., M. Freeman, B. Groom, and F. Nesje. 2015. "Discounting Disentangled." Grantham Research Institute on Climate Change and the Environment Working Paper 172. London: London School of Economics.

Eeckhoudt, L., and H. Schlesinger. 2006. "Putting Risk in Its Proper Place." *American Economic Review* 96(1): 280–9.

Ellsberg, D. 1961. "Risk, Ambiguity, and the Savage Axioms." *Quarterly Journal of Economics* 75: 643–69.

Epstein, L. G., and S. Zin. 1991. "Substitution, Risk Aversion and the Temporal Behavior of Consumption and Asset Returns: An Empirical Framework." *Journal of Political Economy* 99: 263–86.

European Commission. 2008. *Guide to Cost–Benefit Analysis of Investment Projects*. Brussels: European Commission.

Evans, D. J., and H. Sezer. 2005. "Social Discount Rates for Member Countries of the European Union." *Journal of Economic Studies* 32: 47–59.

Fenichel, E. P., and J. K. Abbott. 2014. "Natural Capital: From Metaphor to Measurement." *Journal of the Association of Environmental and Resource Economists* 1: 1–27.

Fischhoff, B. 2007. "An Early History of Hindsight Research." Social Cognition 25: 10–13.

Friedman, M., and L.J. Savage. 1952. "The Expected-Utility Hypothesis And the Measurability of Utility". *The Journal of Political Economy* 60: 463–74.

Fleurbaey, M., and S. Zuber. 2017. "Fair management of social risk." *Journal of Economic Theory* 169: 666–706.

Gilboa, I., and D. Schmeidler. 1989. "Maxmin Expected Utility with Non-unique Prior." *Journal of Mathematical Economics* 18: 141, 153.

Gollier, C. 2008. Discounting with Fat-Tailed Economic Growth." *Journal of Risk and Uncertainty* 37: 171–86.

——. 2010. "Ecological Discounting." *Journal of Economic Theory* 145: 812–29.

——. 2011. *Le calcul du risque dans les investissements publics*. Centre d'Analyse Stratégique, Rapports et Documents n°36. Paris: La Documentation Française.

——. 2012. *Pricing the Planet's Future: The Economics of Discounting Under Uncertainty*. Princeton, NJ: Princeton University Press.

——. 2015. "Valuation of Natural Capital Under Uncertain Substitutability." Unpublished Manuscript. Toulouse: Toulouse School of Economics.

——. 2016. "The Evaluation of Long-Dated Assets: The Role of Parameter Uncertainty." *Journal of Monetary Economics* 84: 66–83.

Gollier, C., and S. Pouget. 2015. "Equilibrium Corporate Behavior and Capital Asset Prices with Socially Responsible Investors." TSE Discussion Paper. Toulouse, France: University of Toulouse.

Gollier, C., and N. Treich. 2003. "Decision-Making Under Scientific Uncertainty: The Economics of the Precautionary Principle." *Journal of Risk and Uncertainty* 27: 77–103.

Gollier, J.-J. 1987. *L'avenir des retraites : Théorie actuarielle, réalisme démographique et économique*. Paris: L'Argus.

Gordon, R. J. 2015. "Secular Stagnation: A Supply-Side View." *American Economic Review* 105: 54–59.

——. 2016. *The Rise and Fall of American Growth: The U.S. Standard of Living Since the Civil War*. Princeton, NJ: Princeton University Press.

Greenstone, M., E. Kopits, and A. Wolverton. 2013. "Developing a Social Cost of Carbon for U.S. Regulatory Analysis: A Methodology and Interpretation." *Review of Environmental Economics and Policy* 7 (1): 23–46.

Groom, B., and D. J. Maddison. 2016. "Non-identical Quadruplets: Four New Estimates of the Elasticity of Marginal Utility for the U.K." Grantham Research Institute on Climate Change and the Environment Working Paper 141. London: Centre for Climate Change Economics and Policy.

Guesnerie, R. 2004. "Calcul économique et développement durable." *Revue Economique* 55: 363–82.

Guiso, L., T. Jappelli, and D. Terlizzese. 1996. "Income Risk, Borrowing Constraints, and Portfolio Choice." *American Economic Review* 86: 158–72.

Halevy, Y., and V. Feltkamp. 2005. "A Bayesian Approach to Uncertainty Aversion." *Review of Economic Studies* 72: 449–66.

Hall, R. E. 1988. "Intertemporal Substitution of Consumption." *Journal of Political Economy* 96: 221–73.

Hammitt, J. K., and L. A. Robinson. 2011. "The Income Elasticity of the Value per Statistical Life: Transferring Estimates Between High and Low Income Populations." *Journal of Benefit-Cost Analysis* 2 (1): 1–29.

Harrod, R.F. 1948. "*Towards a Dynamic Economics*". London: Macmillan.

Harsanyi, J. C. 1953. "Cardinal Utility in Welfare Economics and in the Theory of Risk-Taking." *Journal of Political Economy* 61 (5): 434–35.

———. 1955. "Cardinal Welfare, Individualistic Ethics, and Interpersonal Comparisons of Utility." *Journal of Political Economy* 63 (4): 309–21.

HM Treasury. 2003. *The Green Book: Appraisal and Evaluation in Central Government*. London: HM Treasury.

Hoel, M., and T. Sterner. 2007. "Discounting and Relative Prices." *Climatic Change* 84: 265–80.

Intergovernmental Panel on Climate Change. 1995. *Second Assessment Report*. Intergovernmental Panel on Climate Change. Geneva: World Meteorological Organization and United Nations Environment Programme.

Jensen, M., and W. Meckling. 1976. "Theory of the Firm: Managerial Behavior, Agency Cost, and Capital Structure." *Journal of Financial Economics* 3: 305–60.

King, M., and D. Low. 2014. "Measuring the 'World' Real Interest Rate." NBER Working Paper 19887. Cambridge, MA: National Bureau of Economic Research.

Klibanoff, P., M. Marinacci, and S. Mukerji. 2005. "A Smooth Model of Decision Making Under Ambiguity." *Econometrica* 73: 1849–92.

Koopmans, T. C. 1960. "Stationary Ordinal Utility and Impatience." *Econometrica* 28(2): 287–309.

Krüger, P., A. Landier, and D. Thesmar. 2015. "The WACC Fallacy: The Real Effects of Using a Unique Discount Rate." *Journal of Finance* 70: 1253–85.

Laffont, J.-J., and J. Tirole. 1993. *A Theory of Incentives in Procurement and Regulation.* Cambridge, MA: MIT Press.

Lebègue, D. 2005. *Révision du taux d'actualisation des investissements publics.* Paris: Commissariat Général au Plan.

Le Bris, D., N. Goetzmann, and S. Pouget. 2015. "Testing Asset Pricing Theory on Six Hundred Years of Stock Returns: Prices and Dividends for the Bazacle Company from 1372 to 1946." Discussion Paper. New Haven, CT: Yale University.

Leland, H. E. 1968. "Saving and Uncertainty: The Precautionary Demand for Saving." *Quarterly Journal of Economics* 82(3): 465–73.

Lucas, R. 1978. "Asset Prices in an Exchange Economy." *Econometrica* 46: 1429–46.

Martin, I. 2013. "Consumption-Based Asset Pricing with Higher Cumulants." *Review of Economic Studies* 80(2): 745–73.

Merton, R. C. 1969. "Lifetime Portfolio Selection under Uncertainty: The Continuous-Time Case." *Review of Economics and Statistics* 51: 247–57.

Nordhaus, W. D. 2008. *A Question of Balance: Weighing the Options on Global Warming Policies.* New Haven, CT: Yale University Press.

——. 2011. "Estimates of the Social Cost of Carbon: Background and Results from RICE-2011 model." NBER Working Paper 17540. Cambridge, MA: National Bureau of Economic Research.

Office of Management and Budget. 1972. "To the Heads of Executive Department Establishments, Subject: Discount Rates to Be Used in Evaluating Time Distributed Costs and Benefits." Circular N. A-94 (Revised). Washington, DC: Executive Office of the President.

——. 2003. "To the Heads of Executive Department Establishments, Subject: Regulatory Analysis." Circular N. A-4. Washington, DC: Executive Office of the President.

Pearce, D., and D. Ulph. 1995. "A Social Discount Rate for the United Kingdom." CSERGE Working Paper 95-01. Norwich, UK: School of Environmental Studies, University of East Anglia.

Pindyck, R. S. 2013. "Climate Change Policy: What Do the Models Tell Us?" *Journal of Economic Literature* 51: 860–72.

Pratt, J. 1964. "Risk Aversion in the Small and in the Large." *Econometrica* 32: 122–36.

Quinet, E. 2013. *L'évaluation socioéconomique des investissements publics*. Paris: Commissariat Général à la Stratégie et à la Prospective.

Ramsey, F. P. 1928. "A Mathematical Theory of Savings." *The Economic Journal* 38(152): 543–59.

Rawls, J. 1971. *A Theory of Justice*. Cambridge, MA: Harvard University Press.

Rietz, T. A. 1988. "The Equity Risk Premium: A Solution." *Journal of Monetary Economics* 22 (1): 117–31.

Samuelson, P. A. 1937. "A Note on Measurement of Utility." *The Review of Economic Studies* 4 (2): 155–61.

——. 1969. "Lifetime Portfolio Selection by Dynamic Stochastic Programming." *Review of Economics and Statistics* 51: 239–46.

——. 1970. Economics. 8th ed. New York: McGraw-Hill.

Savage, L. J. 1951. "The Theory of Statistical Decision." *Journal of the American Statistical Association* 46: 55–67.

——. 1954. *The Foundations of Statistics*. New York: Dover.

Selden, L. 1978. "A New Representation of Preferences Over 'Certain × Uncertain' Consumption Pairs: The 'Ordinal Certainty Equivalent' Hypothesis." *Econometrica* 46: 1045–60.

Sen, A. 1973. *On Economic Inequality*. Oxford: Clarendon.

Shapiro, C., and J. E. Stiglitz. 1984. "Equilibrium Unemployment as a Worker Discipline Device." *American Economic Review* 74 (3): 433–44.

Shiller, R. J. 2003. *The New Financial Order: Risk in the Twenty-First Century*. Princeton, NJ: Princeton University Press.

——. 2012. *Finance and the Good Society*. Princeton, NJ: Princeton University Press.

Sidgwick, H. 1890. *The Methods of Ethics*. London: Macmillan.

Solow, R. M. 1974. "The Economics of Resources or the Resources of Economics." *American Economic Review* 64 (2): 1–14.

Stern, N. 1977. "The Marginal Valuation of Income." In *Studies in Modern Economic Analysis*, edited by M. Artis and A. Nobay. Oxford: Blackwell.

——. 2007. *The Economics of Climate Change: The Stern Review*. Cambridge: Cambridge University Press.

Stiglitz, J.E., and A. Weiss. 1981. "Credit Rationing in Markets with Imperfect Information." *American Economic Review* 71: 393–410.

Summers, L. H. 2014. "U.S. Economic Prospects: Secular Stagnation, Hysteresis, and the Zero Lower Bound." *Business Economics* 49: 65–73.

Tirole, J. 2006. *The Theory of Corporate Finance*. Princeton, NJ: Princeton University Press.

Traeger, C. P. 2011. "Sustainability, Limited Substitutability and Non-Constant Social Discount Rates." *Journal of Environmental Economics and Management* 62 (2): 215–28.

Von Neumann, J., and O. Morgenstern. 1947. *Theory of Games and Economic Behavior*. 2nd ed. Princeton, NJ: Princeton University Press.

Weil, P. 1989. "The Equity Premium Puzzle and the Risk-Free Rate Puzzle." *Journal of Monetary Economics* 24: 401–21.

Weitzman, M. L. 1998. "Why the Far-Distant Future Should Be Discounted at Its Lowest Possible Rate." *Journal of Environmental Economics and Management* 36 (3): 201–208.

——. 2001. "Gamma Discounting." *American Economic Review* 91: 260–71.

——. 2007a. "A Review of the Stern Review on the Economics of Climate Change." *Journal of Economic Literature* 45: 703–24.

——. 2007b. "Subjective Expectations and Asset-Return Puzzles." *American Economic Review* 97: 1102–30.

INDEX

social value–maximizing portfolios, xxvii
social welfare, 48; competitive
equilibrium and, 37; evaluation of, 15; function of, 17;
Pigou–Dalton transfer and,
53; social desirability and, 2;
well-beings and, 27
socioeconomic benefits, 158,
159, 160, 170
socioeconomic beta, 157–60, 158
socioeconomic impact, 154
solidarity, 132–34
Solow, Robert, 21
solvency ratio, 79
sovereign bonds, xi, 82, 141
sovereign debt, 82
state-specific gains, 13
state-specific losses, 13
static framework, 23
statistical life: altruism and, 62;
cost–benefit analysis and, 46;
marginal utility and, 111; savings and, 118; valuation and,
61, 117, 158; value and, 51
Stern, N., 166
Sterner, T., 168
stocks, xix, 157
substitutability, 27–29, 109
substitution, 28
Summers, Larry, 51, 52, 84
supply and demand, 72

technocrats, 33
technology: advancement of,
125–26; climate change and,
169; marginal productivity

and, 159; secular stagnation
and, 87
terrorism, 49
Thesmar, D., 160
Tirole, J., xiii, 43, 133
Toulouse School of Economics, 4
trade gains, 60
Treasury bonds, 82, 155
Trump, Donald, xix, 179
Tversky, Amos, 8

uncertainty, xxix; Brownian
and, 149; catastrophic events
and, 113; climate change and,
171; cost–benefit analysis
and, 176; deepness of, 103–9;
economic growth with,
103–4; environment and,
118–19; fossil fuels and, 119;
future generations and, 89,
165; health and, 172; income
and, 89; independence axiom
and, 6; inequality and, 22;
learning and, 169, 170–71;
moral principle and, 4; prudence and, 86–93; risk-free
discount rate and, 135; zero
lower bound and, 115
unemployment, xii, 39
United Nations Climate Change
Conference (COP 21), 68
unweighted, 35
utilitarianism, 20; cost–benefit
analysis and, 15–16; independence axiom and, 21;
intergenerational welfare
and, 136; veil of ignorance